# SEGA

## THE MAURITIAN FOLK DANCE

by

Jacques K. Lee

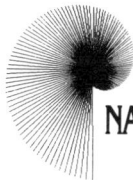

NAUTILUS PUBLISHING CO.

Published by Nautilus Publishing Co.
2a Vant Road
London SW17 8TJ
England
Tel: 081-767 2439
Fax: 081-767 5265

First Edition 1990

ISBN 0 9511296 1 9

© Jacques K. Lee 1990

Front cover photograph: *Ruma Luckeenarain and Alex
Ollivier dancing their way to the UK Sega Championship
1985.*                              Photo: K. Ungapen

Back cover photograph: *A session of séga typique
somewhere on a beach in Mauritius. The beating of the
drums has summoned the dancers and in the flickering
firelight the women waft their colourful skirts to entice the
men to join them — a Mauritian way of asking: Will you
dance with me?*                     Photo: R. J. S. Lee

Printed by The Ludo Press Ltd, London SW18 3DG

2

# DEDICATION

This book is dedicated to Alphonse Ravaton, MBE, better known as P'tit Frère, but whose title as the Father of Mauritian Sega is undisputed. It was he who first popularised our sega nearly half a century ago and encouraged others to follow in his footsteps. This dedication is made in this the 90th year of his life.

And to Sir Harry Tirvengadum, chairman and managing director of Air Mauritius. It was the airline's sponsorship of the UK Sega Championships which helped to glamorise the events and popularise sega among Mauritians in Britain.

Over the years, our national airline has also flown sega troupes to many countries to accompany trade delegations, when sega is used to introduce Mauritius to prospective investors and tourists.

Air Mauritius takes sega to those who have never been to Mauritius and flies others who, having 'experienced' our folk-dance, want to visit the country which produces this unique music.

# ACKNOWLEDGEMENTS

I would like to express sincere thanks to everybody who has in one way or another encouraged me over the years to write this book.

I owe special thanks to Babalé and Claudio for their contributions on the recent sega scene in Mauritius. I must also particularly thank Clarel Betsy for supplying me with much information on European developments and for confirming factual details. Much appreciated is the help of Sylvie Luk Tung and Chico Bernard.

I am most indebted to Vivienne Henry not only for her encouragement and support, but also for constructive and critical comments. I also wish to acknowledge Vicki Palacio's kind assistance for checking the manuscript.

I am grateful to all the authors whose work I have quoted but whose names or sources were not available from the material used.

Last but not least I am most grateful to all the businesses which have taken advertising space in this book. The people behind these advertisements are, in alphabetical order: Luc Cheung, Eric Chung, Liline Doudrich, Sylvain Ho Wing Cheong, Harvin Kaumaya, Sir Harry Tirvengadum and Sylvio Zoil.

# CONTENTS

# FOREWORD

Mauritians living outside Mauritius never really sever the link which they have with their home country. It is therefore not surprising that Jacques Lee's book should be about a subject which is probably the symbol par excellence of the Mauritian community abroad: the sega.

Over the past few years Mauritians have become increasingly aware of the musical cultures that surround them and research has already started into sega as well as into other oral traditions, such as Bhojpuri songs and children's game songs.

This book is therefore a welcome addition to the growing literature written by indigenous researchers, that is, by Mauritians, about aspects of their own music and culture.

Readers in Mauritius and abroad will no doubt find this book invaluable for many reasons. For instance, it is well known to most that sega is a generic term which describes the song and dance of Mauritius and other islands of the Indian Ocean such as Reunion, Rodrigues and the Seychelles. However, most will find it difficult to go beyond this description.

Mr Lee's book provides information on topics such as the history, the evolution and the various styles of sega. Born out of slavery in the early settlement days, sega today has moved out of a specific ethnic group – that of Mauritians of African origin – to become part of the rich multicultural heritage of every Mauritian.

I sincerely hope that this book will have all the success it deserves, since it should do much to encourage cross-cultural understanding, which is primarily about preserving cultural differences while learning to respect them. I should also like to add that such understanding of and respect for all our cultures is in line with the Mauritian Government's policy of unity in diversity.

Armoogum Parsuraman
*Minister of Education, Arts and Culture*
*Mauritius*

9

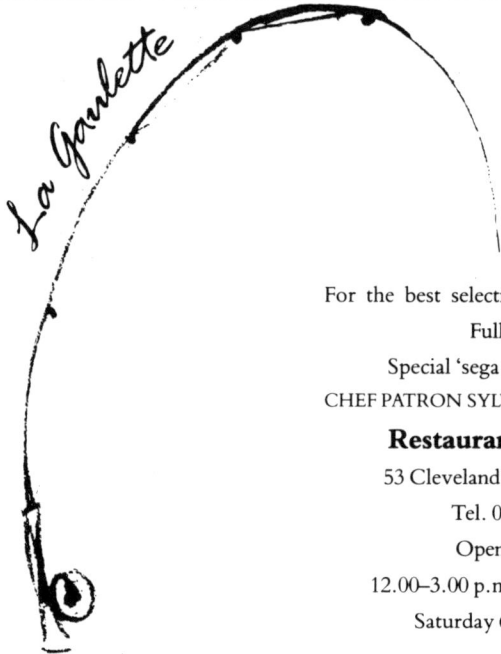

# INTRODUCTION

The idea of promoting Mauritian sega in Britain and making more people aware of our unique folk-dance and music came to me in the early 1980s. I had noticed how many Mauritians had sega cassettes at home which were invariably played at every opportunity. Not being a sega dancer myself, I felt it would be a good thing if others in my position, and especially our children who were born here, could see our sega dance—for it is very much a visual art—and perhaps learn to do it.

I came to the conclusion that the best way to achieve this, and at the same time arouse interest in our sega, was to hold sega competitions.

I had started a Mauritian association with two other compatriots in the 1960s, the Association for the Promotion of the Welfare of Mauritians in the UK (APWM), and at this time it was enjoying a revival with new, dedicated committee members. We were then organising dances on a regular basis as, with our children growing up, there was beginning to be a need for such social functions.

I suggested my plan to the APWM (now a charity: the Overseas Mauritians Aid Trust) and we held the first UK Sega Championship in March 1982 at our Spring Dance. I was then editing the magazine **Voice of Mauritians**, which was read by a lot of Mauritians in London, and decided to use it to give publicity to the competition, the participants and eventually the sega champions. The championship has since become an annual event and many other Mauritian associations up and down the country now organise their own local 'sega night' with a sega competition.

There is no doubt that the publicity which the championship received glamorised it, but its success was also partly due to the top prize. Air Mauritius offered two free air tickets to Mauritius to the winning partners who, once in Mauritius, became celebrities, featuring

11

in the local press and appearing on television. That is why I think our national airline played an important role in spreading sega in the UK. Air Mauritius took over the sponsorship of the championships and today has become associated with the promotion of sega in this country.

Not only have our youngsters, most of them born in the UK, taken to sega as naturally as their cousins back home, but the standard of dancing, especially of those who take part in competitions, is as high as the professional sega dancers in Mauritius.

As is to be expected, Mauritians tend to bring a lot of their non-Mauritian friends to see our sega competitions. And this is where this book was conceived. These friends started to ask their hosts all sorts of questions about sega and these were eventually directed at me!

I decided to write a comprehensive article on the subject that would answer all these questions, and that was when I ran into difficulties. Except for liking sega, and a nostalgia for it which had developed since I left Mauritius, I personally did not know much about sega. I could not find any authoritative writing about it in Britain and further searches in Mauritius revealed that no book had ever been published on it. When asked why, the usual response was: "What's the need? Everybody knows what sega is about."

But that's in Mauritius! We now have a population of over 100,000 'overseas Mauritians' all over the world who may *know* about sega, but that's about as far as it goes. If asked to expand, not many are able to say much more.

Thus began my long search for any material on our sega. I scoured all Mauritian newspapers and magazines to find any reference or articles on sega. I re-read all the books I have on Mauritius and have now probably read most articles written by travel writers who have been to Mauritius in the last decade. I have also interviewed sega singers on their way through London—surprisingly they knew very little about the history of sega!

By the end of 1982 I thought I had collected enough material to write a long piece in **Voice of Mauritians** entitled 'The Rise of Sega in Europe'. The title reflects its more recent development among us exiles on this side of the world rather than its early history back home. But these few thousand words made me an 'authority' on the subject and the article was quoted by many writers and used as a reference source.

I continued to keep up my interest and research on sega and wrote regularly on the subject in **Mauritian International**. I gave interviews on different radio programmes and talked about sega at various events. Over the years I was invited to organise sega demonstrations for all kinds of events from the International Girl Guides 75th Anniversary Rally at Crystal Palace to an open air music and dance festival at Holland Park in London.

I can therefore truly say that if anybody has, I have been sufficiently involved in our sega to write a book on it. And to judge only from the number of enquiries we get at **Mauritian International** for any publication on sega, I have no doubt that there is a need for such a book.

After a decade, I think I now have enough material to publish this small volume. I am the first to admit that it is far from the full story of the evolution of sega. There is still a lot to be discovered; this truly Mauritian phenomenon deserves more intensive research. As I have neither the time nor the experience to do it full justice, I leave it to professional historians to finish the job. If some student or scholar, after reading this book, should be motivated to research further into sega, then it will have achieved one of its aims.

I am confident that **Sega: The Mauritian Folk Dance** has enough in it to answer most people's questions about sega, and I hope it is sufficiently interesting and entertaining to make it a good read. It is aimed at those who, having heard or watched our sega, wish to know more about it without having to read a massive tome. It should be treated as a light-hearted introduction to one aspect of our culture. You will certainly appreciate our sega even more after reading it!

I have no doubt that this book still has some inaccuracies despite all the cross-checking, but I hope there are not too many mistakes: it is difficult to check facts when so little solid information is available!

In order that I may correct any inaccuracies in future editions, I would be most grateful to anyone who takes the trouble to send me any corrections or indeed new information on sega, via Nautilus Publishing Co. It is my intention to make available all material on our sega to any serious researchers.

13

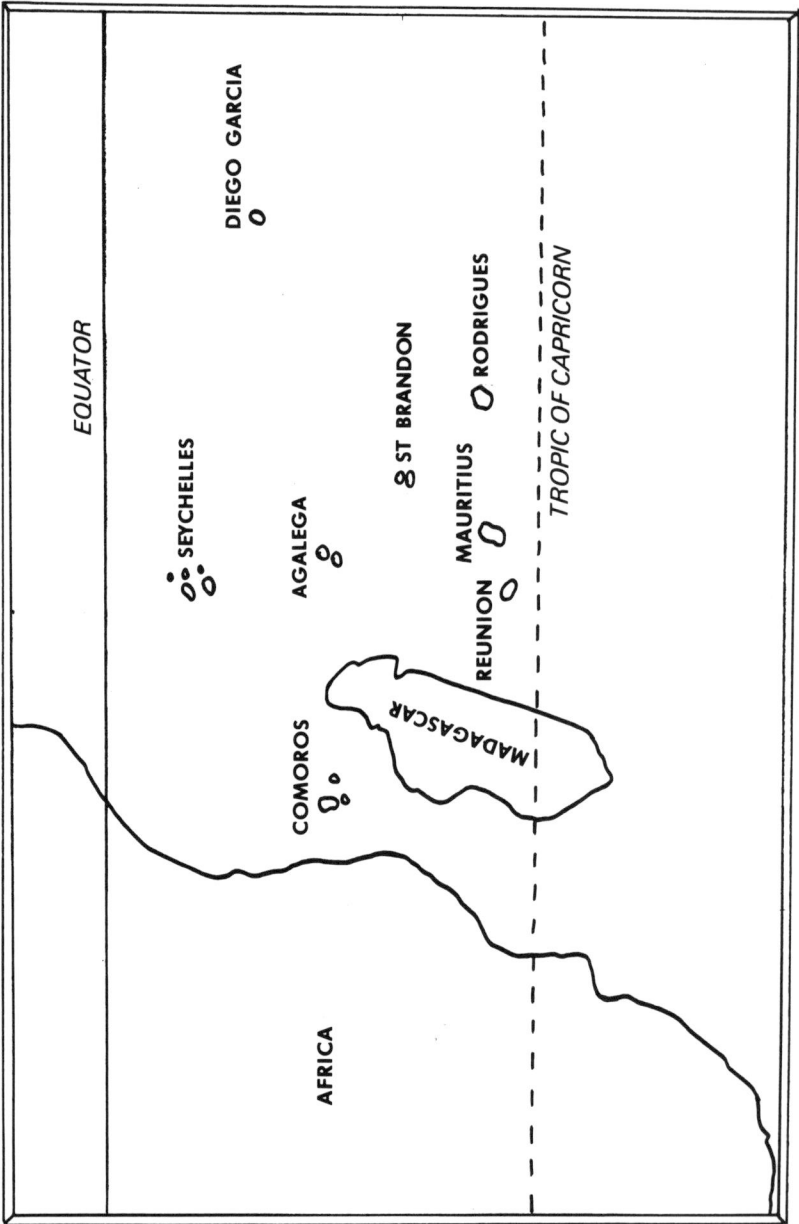

EQUATOR

DIEGO GARCIA
○

SEYCHELLES
○ ○

AGALEGA
○ ○

ST BRANDON
⊗

RODRIGUES
○

MAURITIUS
○

REUNION
○

TROPIC OF CAPRICORN

COMOROS
○ ○

MADAGASCAR

AFRICA

14

# RESTAURANT CHEZ LILINE

## LA CUISINE MAURICIENNE

Liline Doudrich and her two sons
Thierry and Pascal
would like to welcome you
at their family restaurant
WIDE SELECTION OF FRESH MAURITIAN SEAFOOD
Open Monday– Saturday
12.30–3.30 pm & 6.30–11.30 pm

**101 Stroud Green Road Finsbury Park London N4 3PX**
**Tel. 071-263 6550**      *All major credit cards accepted*

See map on facing page

*The islands in the Southern Indian Ocean where you will find sega and their distance from Mauritius. Reunion: 100 miles, Rodrigues: 350 miles, Seychelles: 1000 miles, Agalega: 750 miles, St Brandon: 250 miles and Diego Garcia: 1200 miles. The Creole language is spoken in all these countries. Madagascar is only 550 miles to the west of Mauritius but Creole is not spoken there and sega is non-existent.*

15

CHAPTER 1

# What is sega?

SEGA is music. It is dance. It is song. In fact it is all these combined into one!

Pronounced *say-gah*, it is a way of life in Mauritius. It is a unique sound that, once heard, is forever memorable and instantly recognisable as the music of the island.

Wherever you go in Mauritius the sound of sega follows you. If you are lucky enough to catch sight of this spell-binding dance, stay a while to watch. It is a spectacle to be enjoyed. So just let your eyes feast on it, and if you find the rhythm impossible to resist, join in—you'll find sega a joyful experience.

The pulsating beat of sega is usually accompanied by lyrics in Creole which often have a double meaning or

17

sexual undertones. The words have to be a little risqué really to appeal to Mauritians and they like to know that only they, not non-Mauritians, will appreciate their full meaning.

Sega was originally the soul dance of exiled African slaves. It has developed into something much more sophisticated that is unique to Mauritius and the surrounding islands, and is different to all other forms of music with similar origins.

The dance of sega has been described as a kind of 'symbolic wooing', a courtship drama accompanied by our indigenous music. It is certainly an erotic dance that leaves little to the imagination.

Those who have only seen polished performances of modern sega put on at hotels for the enjoyment of tourists may find the above statement far-fetched. But if you could be on the beach at Rivière Noire, on the west coast of Mauritius where many descendants of the slaves still live, you would see the true sega, and might think differently.

Imagine it is a warm Saturday night, about half a century ago, everywhere is quiet except for the gentle sound of waves breaking on the shore.

Work is done and tomorrow is Sunday so there will be no need to get up early. The local folk are relaxing and want to enjoy themselves. There is no television and, as it is after 7 pm, the *tavernes* are closed.

But there is no shortage of local rum or *alambic* (a crude home-made forerunner to rum) and the villagers gather round a bonfire on the beach to talk and pass the time. Perhaps, more than a century before, their ancestors sat in this same spot, drinking their home-brewed liquor, telling stories and yearning for 'home'. As they relaxed, some would start to sing and dance and others to beat out an exciting rhythm.

These sessions were probably known as *tiéga* or *tchéga*. The modern word sega appears to have first been used in the 1880s. They were what we would today call an open-air party.

This scene was not unusual in that part of the island, even in the 40s and 50s. But what had begun as a local gathering started to attract other people who came to watch the sega on a Saturday night.

Unfortunately that type of traditional sega, or *séga typique* has already almost disappeared. This was classical sega, as opposed to *séga salon*, danced in the houses, or *séga hôtel*, which is what tourists are most likely to encounter.

But to return to the traditional sega on the moonlit beach . . . fuelled by the rum, the villagers become less inhibited, their desire to dance becomes more intense.

The musicians get out their simple goatskin drums, these have a couple of bells attached at either end. They make their way to the fire to warm the drums over the flame to improve their resonance. The men's tight trousers are rolled up above the knee and their shirts unbuttoned and knotted at the front to make movement easier.

The women too are eager to start dancing. They wear full, brightly coloured skirts down to their ankles, and short bodices knotted above a bare midriff.

Other men bring out their 'musical instruments' – a coconut shell or a wooden rectangular box filled with dried seeds; a crude metal triangle, a cooking pot and spoons.

Some may have nothing more than an empty rum bottle which they strike with a piece of broken coral, but even that is enough to beat out the intoxicating rhythm of sega.

Slowly at first, the drums begin, and as the throbbing builds up more villagers come and join the group around the fire. The women are the first to start shuffling their feet and swaying to the powerful beat. Holding out their gaudy skirts in both hands, and swinging their hips, they tempt the men to join them.

In no time, both men and women are stamping their bare feet, abandoning their bodies to the allure of the music, swaying and shaking to the pulsating drums and the tintinnabulation of the triangle and other musical utensils. One of the musicians sings out in a deep, gravelly voice or shouts encouragement to the dancers.

The dancers move towards each other and then apart. At this stage of the dance no-one has a partner, each dancer is alone yet conscious of the others. The women flirt with the men, teasing and taunting them by swinging and lifting their wide skirts. The dancing becomes even more animated and more sensual, the music faster. The dancers approach each other more closely, but never touch.

No wonder that foreigners, seeing these voluptuous women and virile men dancing in such ecstasy, described what follows as a 'simulated sexual act'. A more poetic observer called sega a 'sublimely provocative' dance.

Unable to resist the charm of the women any longer, each man singles out one particular dancer and directs his attention to her, selecting a partner with whom he will reach the climax of the dance.

Some of the men stretch wide their arms as if to catch a partner or to prevent her from escaping. If she does not desire him as a partner or, perhaps, not yet, she turns away. The men go on wooing the women until each finds a partner in a 'contest' which one travel writer described as having all the tension of a musical tug-of-war.

Once two dancers form a pair, they sink to their knees opposite each other, shaking their hips in an erotically suggestive manner. The woman leans back as far as she can while the man extends his body over hers, both moving all the time to the beat of the now frenzied drums. Then they reverse their positions. The man half rises and leans backwards, the woman bending her body above his.

As you picture the passionate excitement of this dance against the vibrant music and crescendo of the drums, you might think that it sounds too overtly sexual and that they go too far. But it is a controlled eroticism. The dancers never actually touch each other during this tempestuous and ecstatic dance. They may occasionally brush their partners in a teasing fashion, but there is really no bodily contact – sega is never obscene.

This final frenetic drumming may last only one minute but by now the performers have been dancing for some 15 minutes. When the music reaches a dramatic climax, on a last, exciting note, it stops – the passion of drummers and dancers spent.

The music has been fulfilled, the climax has been reached. The participants are exhausted, but also stimulated and satisfied by the excitement of the dance. Another traditional sega dance is over.

CHAPTER 2

# The history
# of sega

THE FRENCH took possession of Mauritius in 1715
after the Dutch had abandoned their attempts to colonise
it. They renamed the island Isle de France and brought in
slaves to work in the fields. The first slaves came from West
Africa and Madagascar, and also from East Africa.

Sega began with the slaves and so had its origins in the
countries from which the slaves came. However sega has
evolved and changed, one thing is certain—that its roots
are African. As Jean-Claude Deojec once wrote: *"La
racine africaine du séga saute aux oreilles et aux yeux."*
(One's ears and eyes are struck by the African roots of
sega.)

23

Philip Baker, the acknowledged authority on Mauritian Creole, says that the first visitors to Mauritius to mention the word sega in print were Arago in 1822[1] and Freycinet in 1827 who both called at Mauritius in 1818 while on a voyage round the world. Dr Baker has identified the origins of the word 'sega' as follows:

"Freycinet noted that *chéga ou plutôt tchéga* was the name of a dance from East Africa as well as a general word for tunes composed by slaves. Arago wrote that the *tchéga* of Mauritius was like the dance called *chica* he had seen performed by slaves in Brazil a few months earlier. (The *chica* is also danced in Haiti and Martinique.)

"The spellings adopted by these Frenchmen may seem strange but they were also used by Mauritian writers of the time alongside *tiéga* (Chrestien, 1822), *tschiéga* (D'Unienville, 1838), *céga* (Descroizilles, 1867) and the familiar *séga* (Baissac, 1880).

"The origin of sega is a widespread Bantu verbal root meaning 'play' and, by extension, 'dance'; 'have a good time'; 'laugh'. It is interesting to note that the Creole word has the sense of 'play' in the phrase *pa fer sega ar moi'*, 'don't play around with me'.

"Forms most closely resembling Creole sega are to be found in the languages of East Africa, such as Kaguru sega 'to dance', Nyamwezi *seka* 'to play' and Zigula *seka* 'to laugh'. In other languages of the region, the *s* is sometimes replaced by *sh* or *ch*, thus accounting for variant pronunciations indicated in 19th-century Mauritian texts.

"Further west, in Angola, there are Bantu languages in which the first vowel is *i*, not *e*, and where the pronunciation thus corresponds to the *chica* of Brazil, Haiti and Martinique. Thus the same Bantu root was carried by

24

slaves both west to the Americas and east to the Indian Ocean.

"Not all slaves taken to Mauritius were speakers of Bantu languages. Others came from Madagascar, India and West Africa. These slaves contributed the names of some of the instruments used in playing segas."[2]

We can only speculate as to how sega started in Mauritius and how it travelled to neighbouring islands. It is not possible to say when sega began; there is no definite documentation and in all probability it started gradually and even clandestinely among the first groups of slaves on the Isle de France.

Many of the slaves were badly treated and some managed to escape. These runaways, or 'esclaves marrons', hid in the thick undergrowth which existed then, and lived by gathering fruit, fishing and raiding the plantations.

Both the marrons and the captive slaves must all have yearned for freedom, for home and for the families they had been taken from. When they had a chance to rest once in a while, late in the day when work was done, they would gather together, perhaps around a fire on the beach.

Whenever exiles get together, even today, the talk inevitably drifts to the 'good old days' back home, and the slaves had more reason than most to mourn their lost freedom, their separated families and their miserable lives.

Perhaps with the help of some home-made arrack they enlivened such gatherings by singing songs they remembered from their childhood. No doubt some could make the instruments they also remembered from home, or they would simply make do with anything that served to make some music.

It is not difficult to imagine how the traditional instruments of sega: *ravanne, maravanne* and the *triang* evolved. A piece of dried animal skin stretched over a wooden circle became a makeshift drum. One day, perhaps by accident, such a drum was left too near the bonfire and became quite warm. Hence the discovery that heating the drum improved the resonance. Today *tambouriés* still warm their *ravannes* in front of a fire.

Later someone discovered that by putting some dried seeds in a container, a grating sound was obtained when shaking it. Perhaps the sound so produced was similar to that of an old musical instrument. We now call this the *maravanne* and apart from the wooden box being more colourful and a local bamboo *(fatak)* used for the sides to produce a louder sound, it is basically the same.

There must have been bits of discarded iron rods around even in those days and when these were hit with another piece of metal, they produced a din which contrasted with the other two 'musical instruments'. This *triang* (also called *matriang*), went to complete the trio of what has become the preferred and most widely used means of accompanying the sega. That is, until the arrival of electronic instruments!

As the slaves had come originally from many different tribes and cultures, not to mention countries, this must have presented a language problem at such gatherings. They must also have sung their songs in different languages. Gradually a common language evolved which was greatly influenced by the French slave owners. It was no more than an imitation of the sound of their masters' language, a kind of broken French, but at least it was understood by all the slaves.

With a common language, the slaves could finally sing songs that they all understood. And it was this Creole[3] language which made sega the 'rallying cry' of the slaves and ensured its survival. As the language spread to the neighbouring islands: Rodrigues, Reunion, the Seychelles and other dependencies of Mauritius like Diego Garcia, Agalega and St Brandon, so did sega. It certainly would not have done so if the other countries each had had a different language. Madagascar is a good example. Although it is nearer to Mauritius than some of the other islands, Creole is not spoken in that country and sega does not exist there.

It is quite possible that sega was sometimes used as a medium through which news travelled from island to island. In the days of slavery, the lyrics of the segas were about the people's plight, the cruelty of their masters, their longing for home, the devastation of the last cyclone or perhaps stories about those who had escaped. It was an essential way to express themselves and forget, for a while at least, their sorrows and their back-breaking work from dawn to dusk. Happily, that early music of the slaves is today a music of rejoicing.

Along with the sega, our unwritten Creole language has survived to this age and is the *lingua franca* not only of Mauritius, but also of the neighbouring islands. Regional differences have developed but they are slight and Mauritians, Rodriguans, Seychellois and Reunionnais have no problem in communicating with each other.

Jacques Maunick has written that it was thanks to sega that these lonely Mascarene islands *"ne sont pas uniquement des grains de sable au milieu de l'océan . . . elles ont une âme, un coeur dont le battement s'appelle séga . . ."*

27

("are not just grains of sand in the middle of the ocean, they have a soul and a beating heart which is sega").

Today, along with the rest of Mauritian society, sega is changing fast and it has become necessary to differentiate between the old, traditional form known as *séga typique* or classical sega, and the modern versions.

Moden sega may be *séga salon*, so-called because it is danced in the home (in the living room, or more likely on the verandah) rather than in the open air or on the beach. There is also *séga hôtel* or *séga touriste* which has evolved into polished, colourful shows which, while retaining the essential joyfulness and verve of *séga typique*, have been formalised, choreographed and toned down for the benefit of visitors. Certainly tourists seem to love it – there is nothing like it to break the ice and encourage shy guests to get on the dance floor!

Even traditional sega shows some variations on each island. Rodrigues, for example, is geographically distanced from Mauritius and there has been little outside influence until fairly recently. Also, the population is mainly Creole so perhaps it is not surprising that their sega is very different to that heard in Mauritius. The sega of Rodrigues is called *séga tambour* or *tam tam*, or *séga barré* or *coupé* and the sound is more African and more vigorous than *séga typique*.

*Séga tambour* has the fastest rhythm of any in the Mascarene islands and the sound does not vary much from beginning to end. The same words are repeated over and over again to the insistent rhythm of the drum. As yet, Rodriguans have managed to resist the use of electronic instruments, so the sega is heard in a purer form. In Rodrigues, sega is very often sung only by the women who also do most of the dancing, while the men mainly watch, and take it in turns to join in one at a time. This tradition probably started in the early days of the first settlers when there were far more men than women on the island.

In Reunion *séga typique* is now hardly practised at all and their music sounds more 'French' than in Mauritius or Rodrigues. The *ségatiers* have also abandoned traditional instruments for modern ones and the accordion is particularly popular.

However, it is quite likely that if it were not for the success sega has enjoyed in Mauritius, the Reunionais would today probably be dancing their local dance, the *mayola*. This has to some extent been ousted by the popularity of modern Mauritian sega.

The traditional sega of the Seychelles is slower and the rhythm less strong than in Mauritian sega. But today most Seychellois prefer their modern sega, and the traditional sega has mainly been kept alive because it appeals to the tourists and is often played for them.

Perhaps modern Seychellois sega has moved ahead of Mauritian sega in the sense that it is more like modern western pop music. It is certainly true that Mauritian sega is also moving in this direction.

However, it was in Mauritius that sega flowered into something more than a local folk-dance. At one time regarded as the music only of the 'Creole' people, it became accepted by the whole population and achieved widespread popularity. it has now been transformed into an accepted style of music, which at the height of its popularity in the late 50s and 60s, even rivalled rock and roll on the island.

After the early days of sega the dance suffered a decline. In the first place this was due to the dedicated work of the Catholic missionaries in Mauritius. The blatant sexuality of sega, and no doubt the drinking associated with it, were frowned upon by the Catholic Church. There were also suspicions that dancers became 'possessed by the devil' or that it might be connected with witchcraft. Certainly it was regarded by the Church as an 'occasion for sin' and efforts were made to suppress it, with considerable success.

Another factor was that by the end of the 19th century the majority of the Mauritian population was of Indian origin, who also disapproved of sega. It was regarded as a 'bad thing' and looked down upon. Even as recently as 15 years ago some Hindu and Muslim parents regarded it as a retrograde culture and would not allow their children, or certainly not their daughters, to dance sega.

Luckily, all that has changed. Today, some of the best ségatiers are of Asian origin. In fact, some people say that they make the best dancers because they have such a long tradition of dance and such supple bodies.

Today, every Mauritian has 'segability'. Everybody does it, irrespective of age, ethnic origin or class and it is no longer regarded as shameful. Sega has become a way of life with all the islanders.

But if it had not been for the success of ségatiers like P'tit Frère and Serge Lebrasse who popularised Mauritian sega in the 50s, our music and dance might well have gone the way of the dodo. Those early pioneers composed sega with catchy tunes and words which caught the mood of the people. Sega was newly revealed as something truly Mauritian, and went straight to the heart of an emerging nation seeking its own identity.

It was the fact that sega suddenly found a wider audience and appealed to all ethnic groups that led to its revival and the success it enjoys today. Of course, these pioneers were greatly helped by the wider availability of records and record players, radio and, later, television.

The strong rhythms and catchy tunes were the secret of sega's success, but popular appeal lay also in the lyrics. In the 50s and 60s segatiers no longer had to sing about their lost freedom as their forefathers had done. Instead they sang about the women they admired, unrequited love, unemployment, emigration, mixed marriage and so on.

There were also the sexy, daring sega—the more double-meanings and sexual overtones, the better. At one time there were even segas—called séga X—which were so explicit that they were not available openly in record shops.

One popular sega of the 50s—which today would not be quite so shocking—started thus:

"P'tit Mimi, lave ça verre là
Lave zaffaire là
Mette zaffaire là . . ."

Translation will never do justice to these lines but literally it means:

"Little Mimi, wash the glass, wash the thing,
put the thing in."

Innocent enough to a non-Mauritian perhaps, but rather naughty to anyone speaking Creole, especially when sung by a man to a woman. It must be said that Mauritians took a special delight in knowing that only they, and not foreigners, were likely to understand the full implication of the lyrics.

By this time a costume had emerged as 'traditional' wear for sega. Colourful and distinctive, it retains some vestige of the original clothing that the slaves probably wore.

Today the men wear tight knee breeches and a loose buccaneer shirt which is usually knotted in front and not tucked into the trousers. Some segatiers wear, or carry, a straw hat as part of their costume.

As many of the early freed slaves became fishermen, they did in all probability wear their trousers rolled up above the knee so as not to get them wet or in the way. The shirt was probably torn with no buttons, hence it was knotted. As for the hat—well, why not?

Today the women dancers wear a long, very full skirt with which they flirt and tease their partners. Perhaps the skirts worn by the slaves, at what must have been the highlight of their week, had been discarded by their mistresses. It is the skirt which is the most distinctive and colourful part of the sega costume and the way it is handled, lifted coquettishly, and wafted in the dance, is an essential part of the women's allure.

With the skirt they wear a short bodice or blouse with a bare midriff—today some may wear something that is no bigger than a bikini top, but no doubt this is a more recent innovation!

And so a dance that was born in exile, and knitted together the unhappy slaves from many different places, now links the Mauritians of today with their ancestors. Over the centuries this powerful means of expression has survived and become 'our' folk-dance which now unites the many races of Mauritius.

*Mauritius does not have an official national costume. But Géraldine
Pastor, seen here in her capacity as Miss Mauritius at the Miss World
1986 competition in London, is parading, along with other
competitors, in 'national costume'. The traditional sega wear has been
cleverly adapted and, hey presto! we too have a national
costume!*                                      Photo: K. Ungapen

CHAPTER 3

# Traditional sega instruments

THE EARLY instruments used in sega-making were simply made from easily acquired materials and reflect the ancient traditions of Africa and India. If there were no instruments available, musicians would happily improvise with whatever was at hand.

For example, the seed-pods of the Flamboyant tree (known in Mauritius as the *Bouquet banané*) can be up to two feet long and when dry make a perfect rattle. They are still used as such and no doubt have long been used, together with whatever else lay around, to accompany singing and dancing on the beach.

Today, a spontaneous sega session may start up in a Mauritian *taverne* or on the beach, and people will make music just by using an empty bottle and a spoon or a soap box, or whatever modern equivalent comes to hand.

35

School children on their way to a picnic in a chartered bus will sing segas to pass the time. One of the ways they accompany themselves is by tapping the glass window panes with coins! Nowadays such groups will very likely have two or three 'guitarists' with their instruments at the ready!

A good present-day example of an improvised instrument is a children's 'toy' made of bottle caps. This is often seen being used as one of a sega group's musical instruments. It is simply several piles of bottle caps nailed loosely on a piece of wood. When this is shaken or held in one hand and hit by the other, a musical sound is produced. I have yet to discover an accepted name for it but it is usually simply referred to as *capsils* (bottle caps).

Whilst some of the instruments traditionally used in *séga typique* can still be seen, more or less unchanged, they are increasingly being replaced by more sophisticated modern versions. It is not unusual now to hear the most modern electronic synthesisers accompanying the dancers!

According to Claudie Ricaud[4] whilst, in the past, similar old instruments were found on different islands, they often had different names. In view of the difficult and infrequent contact between the islands in the old days this is not surprising. Nor should we be surprised to see that the same name sometimes came to be given to quite dissimilar instruments. Even on a small island like Mauritius, some of the instruments, just like the word sega, have changed names over the years.

## THE INSTRUMENTS

*BOBRE.* This is a crude string instrument. Originally it was little more than a piece of wood with two strings stretched across it which were plucked. The earliest reference to the *bobre* was in 1769 but the writer called it a *tam tam* qv. The *bobre* is no longer used in Mauritian sega, but is still popular in Reunion where it is known as a *bob* and used predominantly to accompany the local dance, the *mayola*. In the Seychelles the same instrument is known as a *bom*, and there is a similar version called a *zez*.[5]

*CATIA-CATIAC.* A coconut shell with seeds in it which is shaken rhythmically like a maraca. Usually simply called a *coco* – or a *catia-catiac*, after the sound it makes. This is an alternative instrument to the *maravanne*.

*MARAVANNE.* Another shaken instrument. Originally this was simply a rectangular box containing seeds or other objects which, like a *catia-catiac*, would make a noise. This instrument has different names on other islands: in Reunion it is called a *kayam*, in the Seychelles a *kaskavel* and in Madagascar it is a *rabola*. The word *maravanne* may have come from Madagascar where a *marovan* (from *marrow-vany*) is a kind of cylindrical harp.

According to Baker and Hookoomsing a *maravanne* consists of two rows of tubes, made from the stem of the sugar cane cut just below its blossom, held in a rectangular wooden frame. The tubes are filled with the seeds of *kolye sipay* – Job's Tears. However, not all *maravanne* in use today are to this specification and there are different versions.

*RAVANNE.* This is the basic, most important instrument of sega. As it was the main percussion instrument used to accompany classical sega it has become identified with *séga typique*. A *ravanne* is a simple drum made by stretching a piece of goatskin over a frame which is usually cut

37

from the Chinese goyava wood. The frame is known locally as *serk*. Traditionally, two pairs of little cymbals or *tinbales* are set into the wood.

According to Baker/Hookoomsing,[6] the word *ravan* (sic) is derived from *iravanum*, the Tamil word for a tambourine, and this is the name which has become most widely used over the last 50 years.

When sega dancers shout '*sofé ravanne là*' they mean 'play it louder' or literally, 'go and re-heat it'. The drum was heated over an open flame so that the goatskin would dry and tighten, thus giving better resonance. Today the *ravanne* has usually been replaced by modern instruments which do not need to be tuned in this way and the *ravanne* has only symbolic importance.

At one time this instrument was called a *tambour rond* – a straight use of the French word for a drum – and it is still used in Rodrigues. Even today, players of the *ravanne* are called *tambouriés*, especially in Rodrigues.

As Claudie Ricaud says, 19th century travellers called the *ravanne* a *tam tam* (cf. English tom tom), a word which Europeans had taken from the Hindi and which had become a generic term for any primitive drum. From the 18th century some travellers to the Mascarene islands loosely referred to any 'native' musical instrument as a *tam tam*. In Mauritian Creole the word has come to mean 'various small drums, generally associated with Africa'.[7]

In Madagascar a similar drum to the *ravanne* is called *amponga tapaba* and is believed by the Malagacies to be one of the oldest drums used by man. Similar instruments are still found in South East Africa and parts of Portuguese Africa.

Ricaud says that in Mauritius itself the islanders have given this instrument several names over the years. For example, it was referred to as a *marvan* by the end of the last century and a *maronvan* by the early 1920s.

*TRIANG.* In the old days this was simply a length of metal bent into a triangle shape and beaten vigorously with anything from a hammer to another piece of metal. It is the source of the tinkling sound heard above the beat of the *ravanne*. This instrument is still called a *matriang* by some people.

The *triang*, the *ravanne* and *maravanne* were the basic instruments used in traditional sega.

*Traditional sega instruments with modern innovations.*
*Back row, l. to r., an empty bottle with a spoon, the* ravanne *(drum) with a* triang *(triangle) resting on it and the* maravanne *(a rectangular box containing seeds). In the front are modern bongoes and a pair of maracas. These last two have replaced the* ravanne *and the* catia-catiac *respectively in modern sega.*

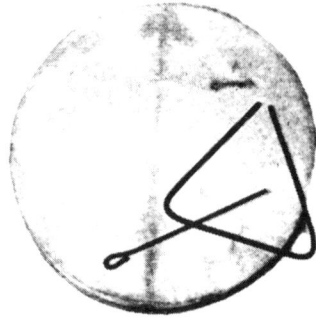

*Some old musical instruments which are now museum pieces. Bottom left, the single-string* bobre; *bottom right*, la serpe—*a cane chopper! Top left is* le banc, *a simple wooden stool which was hit with a club. These three are no longer used in sega. Top right are the famous* ravanne *and* triang *and below them is a* maravanne *and an early version of the instrument.*

# CHAPTER 4

# Terms used in sega dance

## Baré

During sega the male dancer will open his arms wide as if to prevent his female partner from escaping. This is known as doing the *baré*. In *séga typique*, it was the woman who selected her male partner during the dance. If she didn't like the man she was dancing with, she would simply move away to find another. A man who sensed that his female partner was about to go away from him would move around her with his arms outstretched.

In *séga salon* today a man would probably spend all the evening dancing with his own partner but he would still do the *baré* as part of the dance pattern. Some sega dancers would carry a straw hat in one hand for more effect, or even a handkerchief—no doubt because not many of us go to a dance wearing a hat these days!

## Eh-la-eh-la-eh

When the *ségatier*, qv calls *eh-la-eh-la-eh* it is the signal for everyone to join in. As the excitement mounts and the sega reaches a crescendo, this phrase is echoed by all the dancers.

## En bas en bas

When a couple has been formed or 'matched' and the two are dancing together, the man will say *en bas en bas* as he gradually crouches down. He is inviting his partner to do the same and when they are both down on their knees they will take it in turns to perform the *ter à ter* qv.

## Lagam

To *gagne lagam* means to get into the mood. A sega with a good tune is referred to as one which *donne lagam* (gives you the urge) to dance. It has *bon lagam*.

## Sega

The term *sega* is used to describe the dance rhythm, the dance, as well as the music, whether played or sung. Sega is not unique to Mauritius and is to be found in the other southern Indian Ocean islands of Reunion, the Seychelles and in Rodrigues and other dependencies of Mauritius. It has the same meaning in all these countries.

## Ségatier

Originally a sega singer was known as a *ségaterre* but, probably since the 1940s, this has gradually given way to the term *ségatier*. Nowadays the word is used more loosely and is applied to the *tambourié* qv, and to the dancers as well as to the singer specifically.

## Ter à ter

The most sexually suggestive movement in sega. As a couple crouch facing each other, the woman will lean over backwards and her partner extends his body over hers in what has been called 'the copulating position'. As they do this they continue to move and shake their hips with the beat of the music, although they should never touch each other. The couple return to the kneeling position and then their positions are reversed as the man leans backwards with the woman above him.

## Trapé largué

Literally this means 'hold and release' but it is not what you do to your partner during a sega dance! It is the pattern of stopping and releasing the sound of the triangle during play. (See photo of Alphonse Ravaton in chapter 6.)

## Van-vané

In traditional sega everybody joins in and selects a partner during the dance. The men and women eye each other and try to attract each other's attention. The women tease and taunt the men, holding out their gaudy skirts in a colourful swirling fan shape. Waving and lifting the material in a 'come on' fashion they provocatively show their legs, all the while dancing and swinging their hips to the music. This is known as *van-vané*. At this point, some of the men sink down on their knees, perhaps in the hope of glimpsing something more! The next movement in the dance is the *ter à ter*.

During the sega you will hear the dancers call out to each other and some of the things you might hear are: *donne li*—'give it to him/her'; *mo vini*—'here I come'; *causer*—'say something'; *bouze-bouzer*—'move it'; or *ala li la*—'here it is'.

43

CHAPTER 5

# Sega and sex

FOR A long time sega had a reputation for being something of a forbidden fruit. This is understandable, for
certainly the dance is sensual and has a certain eroticism
about it, which is partly what attracts people to it.

The inherent sexuality of sega may lie in its roots. In
many African societies, dancing was traditionally associated
with fertility rites. As sega has its origins in the tribal cultures
brought to Mauritius by the African slaves, it is quite
possible that sega has sprung indirectly from those fertility
dances.

Be that as it may, sega is certainly not unique in being a
dance with connotations of sexual behaviour. Even today,
isn't dancing sometimes seen as a prelude to sex?

Western travel writers who have 'experienced' Mauritian sega never fail to allude to the fact that the dance is sexually suggestive. Descriptions have varied from calling it an 'erotic dance', 'provocative in the extreme' to 'simulated sexual acts'. Several writers have remarked that the dance 'leaves little to the imagination'.

Perhaps most of this sensuality is in fact in the imagination of the beholder. There is no doubt that sega can be suggestive – it is certainly no sedate tea-dance. But the eroticism is always controlled. It never exceeds the limits of decency and is not likely to shock people today. It is not like the *Vaudou* dance from Haiti or the *Macumba* from Brazil which have been described as dances which go to the point of obscenity.

If there is any 'obscenity' in sega it is more likely to be found in the lyrics of the songs. Mauritians do like some of their segas to be suggestive and daring. But this is not likely to shock non-Mauritians because most visitors to the island do not understand Creole, the usual language of sega.

Apart from this, as in any language, many Creole words have a double meaning although they may seem quite innocent to the uninitiated, and sega also uses a great deal of slang. A girlfriend may be referred to as a *zézére* or possibly as a number 17. A singer who sings about spending the night with his '35' is not referring to the number of his house, but to his mistress. (To a Mauritian a girlfriend has got to be young, hence 17, but a mistress should be experienced and mature so perhaps 35 is the right age!)

If we look at sega in the light of 19th century morality, or in the context of the early missionaries to Mauritius, it is easy to see why sega could have been frowned upon, or how stories of licentiousness could have been exaggerated.

The dance, and the rum drinking thought to be associated with it, would have been enough to make any priest raise his eyes to Heaven!

There is, in fact, a great deal of truth in the description of sega which compares it to rum: *"Le séga, c'est du rhum qui se boit par l'oeil et par l'oreille."* (Sega is rum drunk through the eyes and ears.)

Certainly, in the past, the Catholic Church, which saw an inherent moral danger in all forms of dancing, did not view sega with approval. There is no doubt that they tried to suppress it and, along with other sorts of merrymaking, it was banned during Lent. Too much sega dancing till late on Saturday night meant the congregation would not be able to get up early the next morning to attend Mass!

No doubt these prohibitions encouraged the mystique and air of taboo that surrounded sega—and probably contributed to its survival. It is quite likely, too, that its wickedness was exaggerated by those who had witnessed it, to impress those who had not!

Before sega became acceptable, white men went furtively, and without their women, to Rivière Noire on Saturday nights to watch the dancing. Small wonder if those left at home assumed the men went to witness some kind of debauchery. That was why 'respectable' people did not, openly at least, admit to going to Rivière Noire to watch sega although they might go for the 'fresh air'!

Of course the idea that sega was a little daring was, according to the standards of the day, not without foundation. Classical sega is a kind of courtship dance; a symbolic wooing.

The dance begins by the women taunting the men and, when the men respond, the women may reject them

47

by turning away and seeking another partner. Even when a man has been accepted his position is not secure. The woman may tease him or find another more attractive man, changing partners until she finally selects one with whom to sega.

The analogy with sex is further emphasised by the beat of the drum, which starts slowly and builds up in a crescendo to an exciting climax. With inhibitions relaxed by rum or wine, the total effect is compounded by the music and the flickering firelight.

Onlookers, watching this tempestuous dance for the first time, may be forgiven for thinking that things may go a bit too far and prepare themselves for anything. But they need not worry. It is a dance that is in fact controlled and formalised and follows a pattern.

As the beat of the music intensifies, the two partners get closer and closer but, unlike many other dances, in sega the participants never touch each other. There is no denying that it is sublimely provocative, the flirtation real and the movements sensuous, but that is as far as it goes. It is an orgy of music and dance, not an orgy of sex and debauchery.

There is more sex in modern ballet than in sega. In modern dance it has become acceptable for dancers of the same or different sex, often wearing almost nothing or skin-tight, totally revealing leotards, to have complete bodily contact with such suggestive body movements that nothing is left to the imagination!

But calling sega a 'simulated sex act' has to be an exaggeration. If that is what you hope to see you will be disappointed. You would be better off at home watching the late-night movie on TV.

48

When the woman has selected the partner with whom she would like to take the sega to its climax, she will go down on her knees, bending backwards and moving to the rhythm of the music. Her partner will extend his body above hers as they continue to dance together to the pulsating beat, but their bodies should never touch. It is sensual, yes, exciting and joyful, but not simulated sex.

The sega costume has been described as 'sexy' but the women's dress in particular is effective for its colourful and aesthetic qualities rather than because it is revealing. The bodice may sometimes be on the scanty side, but the voyeur will see more on any public beach. Of course, the dancers do lift their skirts to tease their partners, revealing the occasional thigh—or even more—but only in a flash. What is that to the full-frontal can-can?

If sega arouses the onlookers, it is because they are seized by a desire to join in. No one can resist the excitement of the dance or the urge to take part in this joyful experience. Everybody is irresistibly drawn by the spellbinding music—not knowing the steps is no barrier or handicap!

Sega has this effect on people of all ages. You will see little children wriggling their hips to the music as they try out their 'segability'. And there is no age barrier—old people, too, respond to the sound of sega.

Today, sega has truly become a family dance that is enjoyed by all Mauritians, irrespective of ethnic origin or social status. Even priests have been seen to join in the fun. It is a spontaneous expression of happiness.

CHAPTER 6

# Some famous segatiers

IF MAURITIANS were asked to nominate someone as the 'King of Sega' most would choose P'tit Frère. Certainly no historical record of Mauritian sega would be complete without his story.

'P'tit Frère' is the name by which most people on the island know the undisputed father of *séga typique*. He was the composer and singer of early favourites like *Roséda, Anita, Papitou* and *Tire mousoir dans mo poche* (Pull the handkerchief out of my pocket).

I Iis real name is Alphonse Ravaton, and although this name may not be familiar to younger Mauritians, there will not be anyone who has not heard of P'tit Frère. Sometimes classical sega is even referred to as *séga P'tit Frère*.

51

Ravaton is now in his nineties and although he is almost blind, hard of hearing and has difficulty walking, his memory is still sharp and his gravelly voice is quite unmistakable. His well-known face is now lined and worn and he always wears a crumpled felt hat, saying he doesn't feel dressed without it.

He still lives in the little village of Quartier Militaire where he was born. He is quite a celebrity, sought out by many well-wishers who want to talk to him about his long career as a segatier, or perhaps to ask his advice. It needs very little encouragement to get him singing—a tot of rum helps—and he is off!

It is fitting that this simple man who was responsible for reviving sega in Mauritius has not been forgotten. He now talks and sings to visitors he cannot see, but he is honoured that strangers come to pay homage to him as he sits in the shade of a tree, surrounded by his grandchildren and great-grandchildren.

Today P'tit Frère is a respected professional whose talent is recognised by his country. He was the first Mauritian singer to be awarded an MBE for his services to music, and recently his native village renamed a housing estate in his honour, changing it from Cité Padco to Cité Alphonse Ravaton.

Alphonse Ravaton's segas first caught the public's attention in the 1950s and some are still popular today. Like most segatiers, he does not read music, but composed his own segas which, he used to say 'comes on by itself—I compose on the spot'.

His voice was never a pretty one. Mauritians call him the singer with *la voix cassée* (the broken voice). It was his hoarse, rusty voice which earned him the name the 'Louis Armstrong of Mauritius'.

Sega is in his blood. His father was also a segatier and P'tit Frère says he learned many of his early songs from him. Throughout his long life he has lived for this folk music, singing and dancing whenever he had the opportunity.

It was a passion with him, but in his day it was not possible to earn a living from sega. He never made the kind of money that those who followed him were to make.

In fact he always had a reputation for being hard up. This was probably because sega was his first love so he never kept a job for long – and he has had a few in his time! He has been, among other things, a wood cutter, a cane cutter, a watchman, a bus conductor and a stonemason. He did whatever he could to enable him to sing; sega took priority over keeping a job!

Later on, it is true, he also became a fanatical hunter. He will talk to anyone who has time to listen to his exploits at shooting boar, deer, or whatever. He claims once to have shot a record 650 monkeys in just three months. Eventually he had to sell his gun when the licence fee became too expensive. He could perhaps have taken to fishing to satisfy his urge to hunt but he says: *"mo peur di l'eau"* (I'm afraid of water).

Perhaps it is to be expected that someone who preferred making music to having a steady job would always be short of money. One might add that P'tit Frère also had a large family and a fondness for the local rum.

After he received his MBE he is reported to have asked the then prime minister, his contemporary, Sir

53

Seewoosagur Ramgoolam: "Why did you give me that medal?"

"The Queen of England gave it to you, not me," Ramgoolam replied.

"I would have preferred to have been given some money," retorted P'tit Frère.

After that, as he revealed a few years ago, he received a pension from Sir Seewoosagur until the latter's death in 1985.

In those early days of the revival of sega, a segatier could not make a living from the sale of his records. Although P'tit Frère became a celebrity and was known to all Mauritians, he earned very little money from his records. Even his really successful recording of *Tamasa* earned him very little in royalties. He suffered, as many composers and singers do, because much of his work was pirated.

In fact he did not receive his first proper royalty cheque until he was nearly ninety! In 1989 he received an advance payment of nearly £3,000 from Ocora Radio France, who were making a compact disc of his segas, and that was the largest single sum he ever received.

P'tit Frère was not worldly or hoping to make his fortune in the way today's pop idols do. He just wanted to sing and was happy if he had, in his own words, "a little fire to warm my ravanne and some rum to warm my body" then, as he said, "the sega just came by itself."

As a living legend, Alphonse Ravaton was confirmed as the 'grand old man' of sega when, at the town of Curepipe's centenary celebrations in 1990, he was guest of honour at the climax, a *grande soirée de séga*, held at the island's highest point at Trou aux Cerfs. At this open air display, twelve professional sega groups, with about 125 artistes, took part in an extravaganza which proved just how far sega had come in P'tit Frère's lifetime.

In July 1990, Ravaton was honoured in yet another way. The Minister of Education, Arts and Culture Mr Armoogum Parsuraman invited other segatiers to P'tit Frère's home to pay homage to the great man. Among the famous singers who attended and took part in the *fête culturelle* were Georges Armel, Serge Lebrasse, Michel Legris and Micheline Virahsawmy, all of whom said they had learned a great deal about *séga typique* from P'tit Frère.

The Minister also chose this occasion to announce that the newly-founded Conservatoire de Musique François Mitterrand had commissioned a book about Ravaton's life, and that a new cultural centre for sega (a segatorium) was to be instituted by the Centre Culturel Africain.

Mr Parsuraman referred to Ravaton as *un grand serviteur du séga typique*. He also asked him, if he could make one wish, what he would most like to have. P'tit Frère's reply was "An accordion like the one I had when I was young."

"You shall have it," the Minister told him.

The Minister probably did not realise what a task he had undertaken, as Ravaton had played an ancient diatonic Hohner accordion and it seemed that nowhere in Mauritius was such an old instrument to be found. Modern accordions tend to be so complex that the now blind Ravaton would find one difficult to play.

So a national search was begun to find the old instrument and eventually one was found in Rose Hill. It

55

belonged to a Rodriguan who said that that particular Hohner model was still very popular in Rodrigues where it is a treasured musical instrument. Some older Mauritians may still remember listening to Ravaton accompanying himself with an accordion when he sang *Anita* or *Papitou*.

*Alphonse Ravaton, better known as P'tit Frère, demonstrating how to hold a* triang. *With his left hand he does the* trapé-largué, *which is the pattern of stopping and releasing the sound of the triangle. The Father of Mauritian sega was in his seventies when this picture was taken at Rivière Noire.* Photo courtesy of MGTO

# THE CROWN PRINCE OF SEGA

One segatier can perhaps claim to be the crown prince of sega. He was a pupil and protégé of P'tit Frère and his name is Serge Lebrasse. Today, at 60, he is still the darling of sega, and one of the best-loved of all segatiers.

Serge Lebrasse returned to Mauritius in 1951 after being demobilised from the army. He became a music teacher and soon found that one of his neighbours was none other than Alphonse Ravaton who, in middle age, was beginning to make a name for himself singing his own segas.

The younger man listened, and learned all he could about the tradition of sega. He began to accompany P'tit Frère on his singing engagements, learning much from the older man whose talent he admired and envied a little because secretly he yearned to be a singer himself.

It was not long before Lebrasse, encouraged by Ravaton, felt confident enough to start singing himself. Soon he was getting engagements to sing at functions like 'fancy fairs' (local fetes), and beginning to compose his own segas.

One of his first compositions, *Divin lou lou* (Wolf wine), became quite popular and brought him to the attention of a wider public. With his good looks, fine voice and the ability to promote himself, he was clearly on the way to success. Perhaps it could be said that he has another advantage over his rival composers—as a former music teacher he has studied music.

In 1956 the owner of a record shop, Maison Damoo, was sufficiently impressed by the young man to approach him with the idea of making a record. Unfortunately Mr Damoo died before the record was cut.

However, such talent was not to be kept down. It wasn't long before someone else decided to take a chance with the young singer and Serge Lebrasse had an offer from the firm of Ramdharry Frères.

They agreed to make a record with Lebrasse singing one of his own segas *Mama mo le marier* (Mother I want to get married) on one side, and Alex Nanette singing *Eugènie lave ça verre là* (Eugènie wash that glass) on the other.

The recording was duly made and sent to England for the record to be manufactured for release on the Mauritian market. Both songs became well known and popular, but the venture was not a financial success for either promoter or singers.

Part of the problem was that there was no copyright protection and other segatiers sang Lebrasse's songs without paying any royalties. Another factor was that tape recorders had arrived in Mauritius.

While these machines allowed more people to hear sega and helped make the music even more popular, they also permitted them to make recordings from the radio or from borrowed records without having to buy a record at all. Of course, in those early days, marketing as we know it today was non-existent, and it was impossible to recoup the cost of making the record.

In 1957, Lebrasse composed four new segas for the Mr Mauritius National Competition and was asked to perform them as well. One of these, *Madame Eugène*, was to become one of his most successful and popular songs.

By this time he had become one of the most sought after singers on the island, and his segas could be heard everywhere — on tapes or records and people could be heard singing or whistling the catchy tunes all the time.

Another record shop owner, John Venpin, decided to take a chance with Lebrasse and the two got together to cut some more records. This turned out to be 'third time lucky' and the gamble paid off. The records sold like *gâteaux piments* and Serge's position as the crown prince of sega was confirmed. Segamania had arrived.

By the early 60s, Lebrasse had made sega even more popular than rock and roll in Mauritius. He produced one success after another with hits like *Zarina, Sito content moi* (If you love me) and *Bal bobesse* (Candlelight ball).

The last song was not only a success in Mauritius but also in Europe where many Mauritians had begun to play it.

Lebrasse was the first *segatier* to tour abroad. At first it was only to our sister island, Reunion, but in 1967 he was invited to perform at the World Fair in Montreal, and since then he has made many other foreign tours.

In 1989 he sang in London, topping the bill at a concert in Wembley. He sang many of his old favourites to Mauritian exiles, many of whom had not seen him in person since they left home two, or even three, decades earlier.

It was an emotional evening. Over the years Lebrasse has become quite a showman. He has a very likeable personality and knows how to captivate an audience. At Wembley he insisted on speaking Creole, not because he does not speak English but, he told his audience, because only Creole goes with sega—like strawberries and champagne at Wimbledon tennis.

He is well-known for his sense of humour. In 1969, at the height of his career, his sudden death was announced in Mauritius. As the news spread throughout the island,

59

distraught friends and relatives arrived at his home to offer their condolences to the family. Nobody was more surprised than Serge himself to hear of his death, but he was able to joke about it. Following the news of his death he composed a sega, *Kokono pas finne mort* (Kokono is not dead), and one verse goes:

> *Ca même dire ou nous pays*
> *A coté les autres li piti*
> *Mais dans le monde li rénomé*
> *Pou fanne rimère li premié.*

(That's what we call our country
Besides others, it's small,
But in the world it is known that
For spreading rumours it's top!)

But Lebrasse's lyrics can be poetic too, although this is best appreciated by those who know the Creole language which has a kind of picturesque beauty that is lost in translation. Take this verse from *Madame Eugène*, which is reproduced really for the benefit of Mauritian readers.

> *Hier soir, vers le minuit*
> *Lère mo passe cotte cimitière*
> *Mo joinne Madame Eugène*
> *La bouzie rouge dans so la main.*

(Last night near midnight
As I was walking by the graveyard
I met Madame Eugène
A red candle in her hand.)

Two contemporaries of Lebrasse also wrote some memorable segas but did not achieve lasting success as segatiers. Jacques Cantin will be remembered for at least three of his segas—*Mama Bettina*, *Sir Jules* and *Noir, Noir* (Dark, Dark).

The other was Roger Augustin, whose early hits included *Mariage pas ène badinage* (Marriage is not a game) and *Mariage en essai* (Trial marriage). He has since been joined by his son Jean-Claude, who has achieved popularity in his own right. Some of his successes include *Wachiwala* and *Dobi de classe* (High class 'washerman') and *Ou bon mamzelle* (You're a good girl). Jean-Claude is another sega composer with a poetic flair whose lyrics are now being admired for their poetic beauty. He once wrote a poem in praise of Prime Minister Sir Anerood Jugnauth, added music to it and it became another successful sega called *Bravo capitaine*.

In 1976 Serge Lebrasse was awarded an MBE for services to Mauritian culture. There are now two more Lebrasses in the business as his son and daughter have both followed in their father's footsteps.

*Serge Lebrasse in London in 1989. The Prince of Mauritian sega is no longer so young and doesn't dance with quite so much abandon, but his 60s hits were no less appreciated. The predominantly-Mauritian audience at the concert in Wembley gave him a rousing welcome which must have reminded him of his heyday.*

## CLAUDIO

The 1980s have produced several segatiers who have been able to make a name for themselves while remaining based in Mauritius. Among them are Claudio, Jean-Claude, Roger Clency and his wife Marie-Josée, who was the first woman segatier to achieve popular *and* lasting success in her own right. Maria Séga was the first Mauritian woman singer to sing on a commercial basis in the early 50s but she left Mauritius to try her luck in Paris, where she achieved a brief period of stardom.

Claudio is instantly recognisable to all Mauritians by his long black locks which he has not cut since the age of ten. "My hair has become my trademark," he says, "so I can't cut it now!"

His first really big success came in 1980 with his composition *Bhai Aboo* (Brother Aboo). Like many of his colleagues he cannot read music but composes by ear. So far he has over 100 segas to his credit (original and re-worked) and his greatest hits include *Séga banané* (Sega New Year) and *Chérie je t'aime* (Darling I love you).

He is one of the people who has been responsible for the popularity of 'modern sega'. His speciality is to take a well-known song and sing it in the style of sega. "I just give it the sega treatment," he says.

The result is that a popular tune which is well known to everybody is given a new lease of life. He has done this to English, French and Indian songs. He has even made Jingle Bells into a 'sega'!

Claudio's success is due in part to the booming tourist industry. His big break came when Air Mauritius and the Mauritius Government Tourist Office engaged him to help promote the island and tourism.

With his all-female group of dancers called **Satanik** he has performed sega at many promotional functions and trade missions both at home and abroad.

Soon Claudio was spending as much as seven months a year overseas. He has played in most European capitals, but is better known in Africa, where he has had enormous success in Algeria, the Cameroons, Kenya and Zambia. When not touring the world he is based at the Merville Hotel where he sings and catches up with his composing.

Claudio is an exponent of *séga hôtel*. His dancers face the audience and perform sega steps while he sings and moves among them, sometimes joining in the dancing. It is highly polished cabaret and, because it is a rehearsed performance, less sensual than classical sega.

Such shows have a tendency to repeat the same movements and go on a bit too long. It is pleasant to watch as you sit back and relax after dinner but should not be confused with the spontaneous excitement of the true classical sega!

*Marie-Josée, the first Mauritian woman to become a professional and successful solo ségatière.*

*Roger Clency, one of Mauritius' top ségatiers, on tour in London. Joining him in the dance are 'Mauribrit' ségatiers, Mauritians who were born or brought up in Britain. Partnering him in the picture is Yasmin Abdulla, a former Miss Mauritius-UK. Roger is married to Marie-Josée and they often appear together in sega shows.*

## BABALE

Since the 1970s a trend has emerged in Mauritius for segatiers to use just a single name as a professional or showbusiness title. This was perceived as a commercial necessity in a world in which sega is increasingly not restricted to Mauritius, but aims to reach markets throughout the world.

It certainly makes sense when you see the singers' real names! Claude Veeraraghoo has made his name as Claudio; Ruchevilee Modliar as Babalé, and of course, even a generation ago, Alphonse Ravaton made it as P'tit Frère—despite having the advantage of a surname which sounded like an old sega musical instrument!

It would be facile to say that a catchy single or hyphenated name is the main reason for these singers' success but certainly they all seem to have done well. Current favourite segatiers in Mauritius are Babalé, Claudio, Jean-Claude and Marie-Josée, but since the 80s it is Babalé who has been most popular.

A fisherman by trade, Babalé started singing sega in 1978 and, like others before him, his early performances were at 'fancy fairs'. He and his group **Jupiter** sang hits made popular by other singers, but occasionally he would slip one of his own compositions into the programme.

The Mauritian public is always hungry for new segas and the local composers do their best to meet the demand. Most of the songs are short-lived but the first of Babalé's own segas to make a real impact on the islanders was *Difé Bengal* (Bengali fire). It was an immediate success and its individuality was recognised by the Mauritians who kept asking for it.

Babalé's talent as both composer and singer was finally acknowledged and the new success brought him more lucrative engagements and appearances on radio and television. Finally, he was able to make a cassette tape of his segas, and the rest, as they say, is history.

Babalé is another Mauritian segatier who composes by ear, and sings his own compositions. However, he differs from his fellow composers in one respect – he composes at sea!

A fisherman has a lot of time on his hands as he waits for the fish to bite and Babalé uses it to his advantage. He says he would sail far out to sea in his *piroque* (a local fishing boat), for where else could he find such peace and quiet to create! Sitting in his boat he would play his guitar and hope that his Muse would visit him.

He says that even if, at the end of the day, he does not go home with a new sega in his head, he does not usually return empty-handed. His playing and singing always seem to attract an audience and he is sure of a good catch!

Babalé has now had several really successful hits. These include: *Ti crab* (Little crab), *Défaut ti mère* (Little Mum's faults), *Memère* and *Inséparable*.

By 1989 Babalé had a big enough following to make an overseas tour. At first it was just to the Mauritian dependency of Rodrigues, but this was followed by a trip to Europe in the summer of 1990. He sang in Paris and gave so many concerts in major British cities that he must now be almost as well known to Mauritians here as in Mauritius. At the London Mauritian Day in July 1990 he sang to a crowd of between 10,000 and 12,000 people!

Babalé's image is traditional which, for a 38-year-old, is perhaps not surprising. He is clean shaven, short-haired and respectable. No gimmicks for him. None are necessary! Even his costume is not flamboyant. He tends to wear a plain coloured shirt, tucked into his trousers rather than knotted at the waist, and simple breeches which are neither frayed nor rolled up! Of course he does wear the full gear when the occasion demands it.

Babalé is currently working on his latest cassette tape, *Zolie, zolie mamie* (Pretty, pretty Mummy), which is a collection of his most recent segas. It is due to be released at the end of 1990.

## LIKE FATHER, LIKE SON–OR DAUGHTER

It would seem that in Mauritius sega runs in the blood. We know that P'tit Frère says he learned sega from his father, and now his own children and grand-children also sing and compose.

The son and daughter of Serge Lebrasse have also followed in their father's footsteps and are making names for themselves. And Roger Augustin and his son, Jean-Claude, are both famous segatiers.

Michel Legris was one of the people who kept sega alive for several decades without ever making the big-time. Now some of his seven children are in the business and he hopes to see his daughter, Josie, whom he thinks is a natural, launch into the world of international show-business.

He is promoting this talented young lady who has been singing sega since the age of seven and who hopes to become a world-class performer of our dance and music. She got her first big chance in 1989 when she was chosen as a segatiere to go to St Malo in France to help celebrate the 250th anniversary of the arrival of Mahé de La Bourdonnais in Mauritius. (La Bourdonnais was the first and most successful French Governor of the then Isle de France, and a replica of his statue in Port Louis, which he founded, was being installed in his native St Malo.)

A retired builder, Michel Legris now supplements his income by making *ravannes* and claims that his instruments are a distinct improvement on the old ones. They are all made by hand and need only a few minutes heating to restore their resonance, unlike the old instruments which took much longer. He is not revealing his secret technique!

67

Other modern segatiers who deserve a mention are: Johnny Sheridan, France Jemon, Cyril Labonne, Clarel Betsy, Alain Permal, John Kenneth Nelson and Mario Armel.

*The current heart-throb of sega in Mauritius—Babalé. He also has a huge following in Britain since his series of concerts there in 1990.*

Photo P. J. Lee

# CHAPTER 7

# Modern sega

IF A GROUP of Europeans were asked to listen to a record of modern Mauritian sega and then asked from which country they thought it had originated, they would probably give many different answers.

The rhythm, especially when accompanied by guitars, often reminds people of Latin American music. Others may hazard a guess that it is some sort of calypso music from the West Indies. But it would be very surprising if nobody associated modern sega with Africa.

The sound of Africa, in which sega has its roots and which is still strongly identifiable in sega from Rodrigues, may no longer be immediately discernible in the Mauritian sega of the 80s and 90s. This is not just because modern instruments are used, it is also because sega has evolved and changed.

However, if any of the listeners had previously heard *séga typique*, they would certainly recognise the music as coming from the island. In spite of its evolution, modern sega has retained the intrinsic quality that distinguishes it from other forms of music. It is true that it has to some extent moved away from its African heritage, but it is still an immediately recognisable sound which is unique to Mauritius.

There is no doubt that the onset of tourism gave an enormous boost to the development of our music. The islanders discovered that they had something that the visitors loved and wanted. It could be said that sega was there waiting to be discovered and if we hadn't had it, we would have had to invent it. And it is evident that, having realised that the demand for sega was there, we set out to exploit it. And why not?

But sega could not have been invented out of nothing, or in isolation. This music is a reflection of the people and the country and in spite of its changing nature, it is still firmly rooted in our past. It is a joyous manifestation of Mauritian life.

This is one reason why sega cassettes have become such a popular 'export' – for Mauritian exiles as well as for tourists returning home. It's a bit like a postcard in sound, only less likely to be put away and forgotten.

Visitors love to take home a tape to remind themselves of their holiday. English friends have told me that, on a miserable day, they sometimes put on a sega tape, and can be sure that listening to it will cheer them up.

Just listening to sega will get your feet tapping and bring back pleasant memories of a relaxed evening in Mauritius. And, of course, if you have been to Mauritius there is nothing to prevent you pretending that you are still on that silver-white beach in the moonlight, enjoying an unforgettable holiday. If you have not yet visited the island, sega will surely make you wish you had!

It was perhaps inevitable that, if sega was to survive as popular music into the 21st century, it would have to change with the times. It is fortunate that at the same time it has widened its appeal, collected more followers, and travelled beyond our shores.

One problem that could have prevented the traditional sega from becoming a commercial success was its length. A *séga typique* was likely to last about 15 minutes, which is fine for background music, but is not practical if people want to dance to it.

Today, most people listen and dance to sega in their own homes or at parties or functions. However it is played they can only dance for about five minutes at a time. Classical sega was a background for the excitement and pursuit of the traditional dance but because of its length it can become monotonous, however catchy the tune.

Modern sega has a more harmonious rhythm which makes it easier for the uninitiated to dance to, unlike the old sega which has accentuated rhythm. The fact that it is now more acceptable for the dance floor certainly plays an important part in its success.

It was also inevitable that, with the need to cater for much larger audiences, traditional instruments would not be enough. You cannot easily increase the sound from a ravanne, but in this electronic age it is a simple matter to

71

have a keyboard which can produce all the sounds of the traditional instruments and increase the volume at will. Some may be nostalgic for the days of warming the ravanne by the fire, but in many modern settings, it just could not compete.

Increasingly, at public performances of sega, the traditional musical instruments are used more for show than for effect. They have become symbols of sega as a folk-dance, and been displaced for practical purposes by modern ways of making music.

Another reason for their demise is the attraction of modern instruments for other than musical reasons. Today, a big shining, electric guitar is more trendy, more sexy and more redolent of the big time pop stars than something as old-fashioned, or indeed as primitive, as a ravanne. Inevitably young Mauritians, like countless youngsters the world over, see themselves as the next Elvis Presley or Michael Jackson, and to fulfil that dream they need the showy modern instruments, not a box of seeds or an old metal triangle!

Modern sega, using modern instruments, has produced a new sound that record-buying youngsters—not just Mauritians—want to hear. For the last decade or so sega has been handled by a different breed of musicians.

The amateur segatiers like the pioneer P'tit Frère now belong to the pages of history. The modern segatiers are real professionals who have learnt quickly from the music business world of the West. They are not just composers and singers, they are also adept at promoting themselves and their records, and regard the world, not just Mauritius, as their market place.

For a long time now, no Mauritian function anywhere in the world has been complete without sega. At any Mauritian disco, dance or wedding, whether it's in Vacoas, Vancouver, Strasbourg or Sydney, the one sound that's guaranteed to get everybody on to the dance floor is sega.

This is the new commercial sega which appeals to everyone, not just Mauritians, and it is partly through the expatriate communities that knowledge of sega has spread throughout the world.

It has become an export of the country. Tourists, who are almost certain to experience hotel sega during their holiday, like to take some music home with them. But I would urge anyone, if they get the chance, to try to hear and see the original sega in its natural surroundings at Rivière Noire.

As I have said, hotel sega has been refined from the original folk-dance to a sophisticated, colourful cabaret that is pure show business. It has been successful because intrinsically sega has all the attributes of a good musical entertainment, and it would be hard to find a better accompaniment to a barbecue on the beach. Even the story of its origins is a romantic one, and happily the lyrics of sega now tell of happier times than in the days of slavery.

As a musical show it is a joyful display to watch, pleasant to listen to, and hard to resist. It will usually draw the most reticent dancer on to the floor. You do not even need a partner: sega is an invitation for everybody to have a good time!

Two particularly famous holiday-makers would probably agree with that. In 1987 the Duke and Duchess of York spent a holiday in Mauritius which they are reported to have loved. Their hotel, **Le Touessrok**, put on a sega show for their benefit which the young couple apparently found fascinating and enjoyed enormously. No doubt they were given a sega tape to take back with them!

Just as *séga typique* gave way to *séga salon* or modern sega, surely sega will go on changing according to the demands made of it. Today, for example, sega is no longer sung only in Creole. Times have changed and you should not be surprised to hear sega sung in any of the other languages spoken on the island such as French or Bhojpuri; or indeed in the language of any of the countries where Mauritians have settled.

The earliest example of this must be the sega *La Madelaine*. Mario Armel Senior was a popular entertainer of troops while he was on active service in Italy during World War II. He composed a sega with Italian lyrics and it was such a success that even after he returned home he always sang *La Madelaine* in that language.

Soon after Mauritius gained independence in 1968 there was an important development in sega. There appeared what was called *séga engagé*. Loosely this could be called sega of commitment, or political sega. It was something of a misnomer, but the name stuck for want of anything better. The intention behind these songs was to reach the ordinary voters to try to get them involved in the political process.

Mauritians had been told that everybody would be well off once the country was independent. When this did not happen there was great dissatisfaction with the government as the country slid into bankruptcy.

The composers and singers of *séga engagé* were mainly unemployed graduates, politically aware students and other young intellectuals. They had formed a militant students' group – the *Mouvement des Etudiants Militants* which later grew into the political party *Mouvement Militant Mauricien.* [8]

*Ségas engagés* were about unemployment, oppression of the poor, and other political issues. They were played at political meetings and were a great propaganda tool. They were mainly performed by groups such as the *Grup Kiltirel Soley Ruz* (The Red Sun Cultural Group) and later by the break-away *Grup Kiltirel Morysien* (Mauritian Cultural Group).

These groups were a manifestation of the move to Creolise the country, and their lyrics, like their names, spelled Creole in a way that was as unlike French as possible – Creole had, of course, developed only as a spoken language.

However, a non-Mauritian who heard *séga engagé* for the first time would probably say that it had more in common with Indian songs than with sega. And indeed that is what most of these segas were: re-hashed popular Indian songs given a sega rhythm. The only sega instrument used by these groups was the ravanne, otherwise they accompanied themselves with a tabla, sitar, or with a keyboard, guitar or other modern instruments.

But these segas were well received and their popularity lasted long enough for some of the segatiers to make their names locally. They included Micheline Virahsawmy, Ram Joganah, Menoir, Nitish Joganah and in particular Bam Cuttayan. The latter said recently that his form of sega did not survive because "today people no longer have time to get involved in anything".

However, *séga engagé* was more than a passing phase

75

–it made an important contribution to modern sega by making it more acceptable to a wider audience. The songs had a message and were not only aimed at all ethnic groups but were successful in reaching them. They were particularly effective in winning over Indian women.

Much of the credit for giving sega a more 'respectable' image goes to Serge Lebrasse. Until he appeared on the scene sega was regarded as something suitable only for the *basse société* (low class). As a school teacher, not only was Lebrasse the first professional person to be openly associated with sega but he was also its best advocate.

In the last couple of years Mauritius has heard yet another new sound–*seggae*. This is a mixture of sega and reggae! Mauritians in London had already tried combining these two in the 70s but it never enjoyed such popularity.

A local group called *Racinetatane* had been playing in Mauritius for several years–playing not only sega but also reggae. Then a young sega enthusiast, Percy Yip Tong, who had 'discovered' reggae while a student in France, got involved with *Racinetatane* when he returned home.

The result was that the group invented a different style of music which they dubbed *seggae*. It was certainly successful: it is a lively sound, good to dance to, and young Mauritians have certainly taken to it. But whether it is just a fad that will soon be forgotten remains to be seen.

In the meantime, it appears that not just Mauritians, but Reunionnais also like *seggae*. *Racinetatane* were invited to take part in the *Rencontre de Jazz et de Musique Populaire de l'Océan Indien* in 1990 and were also planning to sell *seggae* to the world at large.

Musicians in many countries have tried to combine jazz with other forms of music. The first person to try this with sega was Gaëtan Alkoordoss, although it has not really caught on. It sounds an interesting combination, but only time will tell whether *sejaz* will be as successful as *seggae*.

Sega is part of the roots and history of Mauritius. It is as much part of Mauritian life as the stone-studded cane fields. Mauritians are proud of their heritage and it is surely something they will always cherish. The only uncertain thing about sega is not how long it will last, but how long it will be before it makes a place for itself in everyone's vocabulary, and in the pages of the Oxford English Dictionary!

*Sega provides an ideal entertainment for hotel guests. This is a live show in which they can take part — usually without having to be first invited!*    Photo courtesy of MGTO

*Claudio (kneeling) in a display of modern sega. Unlike séga typique this is cabaret with the singer and his dancers facing the audience. It makes a colourful show but the sheer excitement of classical sega is lacking. There is not one ravanne in sight; instead, they are using modern drums and guitars.*
Photo K. Ungapen

78

CHAPTER 8

# The home of sega

IN PREVIOUS chapters the name of Rivière Noire has been mentioned several times as the home of *séga typique*. If you do not happen to know the area already, you may well be wondering what kind of place it is and why sega should have started in this particular part of the island.

This chapter will take you back a few centuries to the time when the only people you would have been likely to meet at Rivière Noire were runaway slaves—or, more probably, you would not have seen anyone—but they would certainly have been watching you! And we shall see why this region became the birthplace of sega.

Rivière Noire (Black River) is one of the nine districts of Mauritius. It was first named by the Dutch who called it

*Zwarte* after the 'black' water. In fact the river is clear but the water looks dark as it flows over the black rocks that abound in the area, on the river bed, and along the coast, particularly at Tamarin.

It is a long district which starts at the Le Morne peninsula in the south-west corner of the island and follows the coast as it twists and turns right up to the boundary of Port Louis, the island's capital.

In this area, which includes the Rivière Noire mountains, is to be found some of the most picturesque scenery in Mauritius. And unlike the east coast it is sheltered from the strong winds that blow in the winter months, from July to September.

Its connection with sega dates back to the days of the slaves, when the mountain of Morne Brabant was a well-known hideout of the *esclaves marrons*–the runaway slaves.

It was not surprising that the fugitives chose this area to hide. If you venture to Plaine Champagne, just a few miles north of Morne Brabant, you will find a part of Mauritius that has remained almost unchanged since the days of the Dutch occupation in the 17th century. The thick under-growth and forest provided an ideal hiding place into which their French masters dared not go, or could not easily have hunted for the runaways.

In this area there were wild pigs which had escaped from the early Portuguese merchant ships, and Javanese deer which had been introduced by the Dutch. Not far away is Montagne Jaquot (Monkey Mountain) where the slaves would have found monkeys to hunt for food.

Unfortunately the dodo had already been exterminated

by then, or they could have caught these tame birds by hand–although history books tell us that they did not make very good eating!

Wild fruit trees were in even greater abundance than they are today and would have provided the slaves with much that they needed, even if it fell short of the paradise described in *Paul et Virginie*.[9]

They had only to share these fruits of the forest with the myriad beautiful birds, the monkeys and large bats or flying foxes. The Chinese goyava trees are particularly plentiful in that region to this day, so perhaps that is why the wood was chosen for the frame of the ravanne.

It is true that the runaway slaves had a reputation for being marauders who pillaged plantations and killed the planters' livestock, but this was probably in order to exact revenge for the cruelty of their former masters, and not because they were starving.

There is no shortage of water in the region, for apart from Rivière Noire itself, there is a pool at the bottom of the spectacular Chamarel waterfall and nearby there are the smaller Alexandra Falls. There were also streams, and some small lakes which are today used as reservoirs.[10]

Being some 700 metres above sea level, with shady trees and soft sea breezes, it must have been a cool place to be during the heat of the day. From the heights of Plaine Champagne the slaves would have had an amazing panoramic view and been able to keep a look-out over the astounding gorges of the Rivière Noire. This was then the natural habitat of the Mauritian kestrel, now one of the world's most threatened birds.

The area also includes a strange geological curiosity–

81

the volcanic remains at Chamarel where the earth is exposed in seven distinct colours. The Mauritians would like to believe they can see the colours of the rainbow in the coloured earth, echoing the new symbol of the island as *la nation arc-en-ciel* (the rainbow nation).

If the *marrons* wanted a change of diet, Black River Bay is rich in fish even today and it is from here that most deep sea fishing expeditions now start. When they dared venture into the open spaces of the beach, the slaves would have found abundant fish, and perhaps picked up the enormous shells of the giant clam in which to store their water. They could have found hiding places, and perhaps protection from the cyclones, in some of the largest caves on the island. Pointe-aux-Caves and Trois Cavernes are today tourist attractions, but don't believe anyone who tells you that the caves stretch under the sea as far as our sister island, Reunion!

So it was along the beaches of Rivière Noire, where these first Mauritians gathered round their fires in the evenings to sing and dance, that sega has its roots. Perhaps, they believed their motherland was just across the sea beyond the horizon and directed their plaintive song at their homes.

The British captured Isle de France from the French in 1810 and re-named it Mauritius, its former Dutch name. They abolished slavery on the island in 1835 and many of the freed slaves then made their way to Rivière Noire, perhaps because they had heard about the area, or its wilderness reminded them of home. No doubt they felt there was safety in numbers and it was still a place the white settlers avoided.

The British Government sent a group of soldiers to

Morne Brabant to inform the runaway slaves that they need no longer hide. Being accustomed to fleeing at the sight of white men in uniform, some of the terrified runaways mistakenly believed they were about to be recaptured, and rather than risk a return to slavery, they jumped to their death from the summit. They plunged over a sheer cliff some 550 metres high, and there is still a cross there to mark this tragic event in Mauritian history.

The sega of Rivière Noire is not the only link with the past. The little village of Case Noyale is a poignant reminder of the dangerous days of slavery. It takes its name from the house of a French soldier called Noyale who was murdered there by one of the *marrons*.[11]

The district of Rivière Noire today has some 30,000 inhabitants who are mostly descendants of the slaves, and this region could be described as the most 'African' part of Mauritius.

Most of the arable land in the area is now under sugar, and where sugar will not grow there are plantations of coconuts and coffee. There is also a nature reserve and in the north, at Tamarin, salt is produced in large square salt pans.

As in other rural parts of the island, many of the local inhabitants of Rivière Noire work in the sugar industry. But many make their living from fishing, especially from January to June when the sugar cane is growing and there is not much work in the mills.

It is here that the huge marlin fish are brought back by triumphant international teams of deep-sea fishermen to be smoked in the nearby village of Wolmar. The charcoal used is also produced in the neighbouring forest.

83

Some of the fishermen now fish exclusively for the local hotels which also employ many of the villagers. Rivière Noire has not changed a great deal over the centuries and it is clear why it is now such a favourite place for tourists. If you are ever tempted to spend a holiday in Mauritius, you may well stay on this west coast as some of the best-known hotels are here, near Flic-en-Flac, which is known as the 'Riviera' of Mauritius.

By the end of the last century the freed slaves had become integrated with the rest of the population but would still gather to sing and dance their sega round a fire on the beach near their homes. Because they no longer had to do it clandestinely, they were able to express themselves more freely and the classical sega as we know it today probably developed at this period.

Over the years their music, and especially their erotic dance, drew people from far and wide to watch them. Today this region is famed as the home of the authentic folk-dance of Mauritius. The island to which they were once taken by force has become their home and a place of peace. Rivière Noire is now a favourite refuge for the many visitors who fly thousands of miles in order to get away from the pressures of modern life.

So when *you* go to the island on holiday, do not be content just to watch the *séga hôtel* by professional segatiers put on for your benefit, be more adventurous – go out and watch the villagers of Rivière Noire. Only then can you say: "I have experienced the real sega of Mauritius."

# CHAPTER 9

# Sega in Europe

THE CREDIT for introducing Mauritian sega to Europe must go to Gaëtan de Rosnay. A Frenchman with Mauritian ancestry, he was involved in the making of Louis Malle's film *Les Amants* which featured sega. That was in the early 60s, and was probably how French cinemagoers first caught a glimpse of our folk-dance.

In Mauritius, segamania was at its height and some of the more ambitious segatiers had already left home to try their luck at singing sega in France. With the long cultural association between France and Mauritius, it seemed the natural place to go.

Maria Séga and Gilles Sala were probably the first Mauritians to try to enter the popular music scene in Paris where singers like Luis Mariano, Tino Rossi, Gilbert Bécaud and Edith Piaf were performing—the stuff Mauritian dreams were made of.

Maria Séga, whose real name was Marie Germaine, was not only beautiful, but also a talented singer and dancer. She was the first Mauritian female singer to appear on the stage professionally, but she left for Paris before she could become a household name on the island.

She arrived in Paris in the early 50s as "the exotic and beautiful sega singer from Ile Maurice". She sang in French —not in the colourful long skirt that we now associate with sega but in something like a short, tight saree that owed more to the fashions of the time. But she soon found that the French were not yet ready for her music.

However, she persevered and did make a few records in France which people may still remember. The most popular was probably *La Pointe-aux-Piments*, an old Mauritian song which she turned into a sega, although it must be said that the sega treatment was a very mild one.

She did achieve a little of the fame she had hoped to find in France, appearing on a TV show in 1957, but her success was shortlived and she returned to Mauritius in 1962. Later she went to Madagascar to start a new life, and there she married a Frenchman, Eugène Varlez.

Not many people in Mauritius would remember Maria Séga today had it not been for the visit to the island of François Mitterrand in June 1990.

Back in Mauritius, the Varlezs had started a correspondence with the Mitterrands which was reciprocated. After Eugène Varlez died in 1987 the correspondence continued and Maria kept in touch with the Mitterrands, although they never met.

When the French President and his wife visited the island, Maria Varlez was finally introduced to them, but she did not sing for them, that honour went to the segatier Serge Lebrasse.

Of course, there were other reasons why sega did not succeed in France in the 60s: it was a time of great ferment in the pop world. It was the era of the Beatles and the Rolling Stones and the music world at that time was immensely competitive. Sega was a completely different sound and France, like most of Europe, was already totally taken up with the explosion in pop music.

Perhaps Maria Séga's mistake was to try to tone down her sega for the French, depriving her songs of the original rhythm and vigour. If she had sung in Creole she might have kept her air of exotic mystery rather than sound like an imposter singing in French. The later success in France of segas sung in Creole without any modification proves this point. As Mauritian Creole is three-quarters French, French speakers claim they have no problem understanding it.

France has always maintained close ties with Mauritius. Air France had a weekly flight to the island long before any other airline thought it worthwhile to operate the route. For this reason and because of our historic ties, the French have always formed the majority of our foreign visitors and this has been important in spreading sega in France.

The visitors hear and see sega in its natural surroundings and ask for sega when they get back home. They took readily to the traditional music and by the early 80s it was no longer a strange sound but part of the popular music scene. The albums on sale in France are not usually made in a studio there, but are recorded live in Mauritius, and sega is appreciated for what it is—part of Mauritian culture.

The popularity of sega in France encouraged some of our best singers to emigrate there. A few have been really successful and others find they can make a good living. Many of them have ended up modifying their style, singing in both French and English and widening their repertoire to include other styles of music.

Interestingly, these exiles have never been able to compete with the segatiers who have remained in Mauritius. Perhaps the natural surroundings of sega—a combination of sun, sea and rum—are an essential background to achieve the true spirit of sega! Or perhaps sega in its purer form is just that much better?

Some of the people who have 'made it' in France are Clarel Betsy, Cyril Labonne, Gaëtan Valentin, Alain Permal and Johnny Sheridan (whose real name is Jean-Claude Permal, brother of Alain).

Johnny Sheridan has been in Europe since 1972 and is probably one of the most successful of this group. It was he who composed and sang the sega in Ramesh Tekoit's first Mauritian film, *Et le sourire revient* (And the smile returns), which had its première in Paris in 1980.

Another segatier who has been very successful in France is Clarel Betsy. He first made his name in 1970 when his record *Plastic girl* was a big hit in Mauritius. As a result he decided to look for bigger audiences and went to Europe the following year.

Today, although some of his segas sell quite well in Mauritius, it is in France that he is best known as a popular singer. So far Betsy has written over one hundred songs and has made about 20 albums, not to mention another 50 records and a dozen cassettes.

The most recent person to promote sega in France is not a Mauritian but a regular visitor to the island who has fallen in love with Mauritius and its people and has a passion for our sega: Princess Stephanie of Monaco.

In 1987 she had ambitions to be a pop singer and brought out an album which included a few sega numbers. She described them as her 'homage to Mauritius'.

Mauritians who have heard her songs say they bear little resemblance to genuine sega, but perhaps these critics have a prejudice against a non-Mauritian interpreter! Nevertheless sega received a great deal of publicity when her record was released and she appeared on television dancing the sega. No-one criticised her dancing. After so many visits to Mauritius it must be admitted she can dance sega as well as any native islander.

The earliest serious attempt to promote sega in Britain was probably in 1968. Two brothers, Tyrone and Denver Mayard, and a couple of friends, made a sega record in Creole called 'Doris'. But despite the valiant efforts of their then 'manager', an English friend called Paul Draper, it did not get very far.

Paul Draper had developed a great love for our sega. Before even setting foot in Mauritius he spoke Creole so well that friends used to pass him off as a Mauritian.

Eventually, in 1974, Paul did get to Mauritius for a holiday—and stayed for good. In fact he made the island his home and took Mauritian nationality. He is now the director of **Craft Aid**, which he founded to provide residential accommodation and employment for disabled people. However, he has kept up his interest in popular music, especially sega, and until recently he was a disc-jockey for two record programmes on Mauritian radio.

Then in the early 70s, three London-based brothers, Jean-Antoine, Mario and Chico Bernard, together with Daniel Bêche and Noël Cécile formed a sega group called **Creolites**. Like many similar groups in Britain in those days they played in pubs, and for weddings and similar events, just earning enough to cover their expenses.

However, in 1974, **Creolites** hit the headlines in Mauritius when a sega record they had made privately began to sell well on the island. The songs were *Immigrants débarqués* (Disembarked immigrants) and *Regsega Kung Fu*, the latter is a mixture of sega and blue beat which was then becoming known as reggae. They did not sell many copies in Britain, but in Mauritius the youngsters loved *Regsega Kung Fu* and bought nearly 15,000 records—enough to take it to the top of the local pop chart. But by the end of the 70s the group had split up.

Two other Mauritian groups which included sega in their repertoire were the **Mascarenhas** and **The Dragons**. The latter was very professional and one of the most successful Mauritian groups in London, lasting until the mid-80s.

This group also consisted of three brothers: Cyril, Gerry and Louis Chan Lok, and their brother-in-law, Colen Raman. They played to royalty, won the Pub Entertainer of the Year Award in 1979 and finished second in the TV competition **Opportunity Knocks**. Although they were not true segatiers, they often played sega.

When 'discos' started to become popular, the organisers of Mauritian dances who had been engaging live bands to play sega began to save money by playing records instead. Another advantage of discos was that the dancers could hear all the latest sega hits sung by the segatiers themselves, and this helped to boost their popularity in Britain.

Over the last few years Mauritians living in London have composed a few segas, some in Creole and some in English, which they have made into records or cassettes. One which achieved some success was *Pas bizoin plorer* (There's no need to cry) by Gary Appapoulay.

In Britain the tape was bought mainly by the Mauritian community but it sold even better in France and Reunion. However, the record's greatest success was in Mauritius, where it got to be No. 3 in the pop chart.

Gaby was once known as 'King Creole' in Mauritius. He was beginning to make a name for himself there as a singer and composer of segas and popular songs when he decided to come to Britain to study. However, he eventually dropped out of university, not because he was spending too much time making music, but because he had got married and had a family to support. Today his children are all musicians and have their own band which plays regularly.

The longest-lasting Mauritian group in London is the **Zoil Foundation** whose 12 members are all brothers and sisters! The group started life as just another pop group but over the last few years has begun to specialise in sega, using traditional instruments. They have brought out their own sega record and now not only play modern sega, but also put on shows of *séga typique* complete with dancers in traditional sega costume.

Since the UK Sega Championship was launched in 1982 there is no doubt that, among the expatriate Mauritian community, sega has enjoyed a revival and has

91

become the most important cultural link with home. It is also something that brings all Mauritians together.

The first championship took place in London and was won by Pauline Vincent and Anwar Aumjaud. They were two friends who took sega seriously and had spent months prior to the competition practising their technique.

Their win was significant in another respect. It testifies to the fact that today sega is enjoyed by all Mauritians and knows no ethnic barriers—Pauline is Creole and Anwar a Muslim Mauritian. The current sega champions are two cousins, Sylvie Luk Tung and Jean-Eddy Luk Tung. Since winning Sylvie has not stopped dancing; she has formed her own dance group and has been kept very busy performing all over the country.

In the last few years the country has seen many public demonstrations of sega, from a display at Waterloo Station to the TV programme **Blue Peter**. The one at the international World Travel Market was so popular that it should become an annual feature. But perhaps our folk-dance received its most extensive publicity when it was included in the 1986 Lord Mayor's Show, ensuring national TV coverage.

That evening the newly-installed Lord Mayor of the City of London, Sir David Rowe-Ham, did Mauritius a great honour by having sega to entertain his guests at a reception on **HMS President** on the river Thames. Beneath a sky alight with a thousand fireworks, the sound of sega vibrated through the ship and as the dancing ended, Sir David told his guests: "Now you know why I keep going to Mauritius for my holidays!" He added that he could not remember whether his forthcoming visit would be his tenth or eleventh stay on the island.

For Mauritians who wanted to enjoy sega regularly, Jocelyn Salomon opened a Sega Club in north London in the mid-80s. It is not exactly Rivière Noire but members can listen to the latest sega recordings and sometimes there are live shows by Mauritian segatiers.

There is now sufficient demand for sega in the UK to make it worthwhile for sega artistes to come to perform in Britain. In 1989 a young Mauritian entrepreneur, Cass Rawat, organised a 'sega extravaganza' at Wembley and brought four top segatiers from Mauritius to appear at the show. It was not a financial success for the organisers, but it was perhaps a little over ambitious! One famous segatier at a time would keep sega fans quite happy.

*Séga typique in England. From left to right: Sylvie Luk Tung and Richard Dowlet have formed a pair. They raise their arms as if to embrace each other but bodily contact is not allowed! He is doing the* baré, *trying to prevent her getting away or being enticed away by another dancer. Ruma Luckeenarain (centre) has not yet chosen a partner, while next to her, Brigitte Roussel turns away to find another dancer, she ignores the attentions of Jacques Roussel (far right) who does the* baré *to stop her from escaping, but it is too late!* Photo K. Ungapen

*The famous dome of St Paul's Cathedral confirms that the segatiers atop the float are in the City of London—taking part in the Lord Mayor's Show. The British policeman is trying hard not to appear to be moving his arms to the pulsating sound of sega music.*

Photo courtesy Air Mauritius

# CHAPTER 10

# The future of sega

SEGA has not yet produced a 'megastar' of international stature and perhaps that is what is needed if sega is to achieve the kind of worldwide success that many sega enthusiasts believe it deserves.

Someone who could become a world-class star as an exponent of sega is what is necessary to really capture the public's attention – another Harry Belafonte or Bob Marley! And yet, it is realistic rather than cynical to recognise that even a brilliant and charismatic performer has got to be marketed properly. Today, talent is not enough. The right backing and excellent PR are essential if a performer is to make any headway in the world of modern music.

95

If megastars have to be 'manufactured' there still has to be a bedrock of talent and a thriving interest in sega from which a star can emerge. If Mauritian folk-dance is to have a truly international appeal the country must provide the right conditions in which sega can be kept alive in its purest form, and in which local talent can be nurtured.

So far there is not a single place that can be a focus for sega. We keep returning to Rivière Noire as the birthplace of our folk-dance, but as sega becomes accepted as the heritage of all Mauritians, perhaps we should be looking forward, and making sure that the true living sega is available to everyone.

The 'segatorium' to be built at the *Centre Culturel Africain* is a beginning. Sega should have a home that can become a centre of knowledge and excellence, an archive and museum, and a place where people can come to learn about sega as well as watch and hear the best practitioners available.

Perhaps only the best performers should be good enough to appear at the segatorium. It should become the place that youngsters aspire to: performing there would be an accolade to be earned. It is to be hoped that there will also be courses available, and facilities for those who wish to study all aspects of sega.

With the opening of the segatorium perhaps we should consider the creation of an Academy of Sega whose role would be to maintain standards and to ensure that traditional sega is preserved in its purest form.

We have seen how sega has changed over recent years by absorbing outside influences from other types of music, and how is has been adapted and modified to meet the demands of modern taste.

While it is true that these changes have widened the appeal of sega and contributed to the health of our music, they are likely in the long run to obliterate the traditional *séga typique* unless we make a conscious effort to preserve it. This should be the role of an Academy.

Perhaps this body should be empowered to prohibit the use of the term 'sega' to describe any song that does not comply to a set standard, and act as a sort of watchdog to ensure that insidious changes do not occur.

For example, today segatiers keep inventing terms associated with sega: a ravanne player is now sometimes referred to as a *ravannier* or a triangle player as a *trianglist* — expressions which were not used in the past.

While it must always have been the case that folk-dance grew and developed, the difference now is that it is exposed to outside influences. What is needed is a determined effort to preserve the traditional sega so that it can keep its distinctive, historic character rather than, chameleon-like, reflect other forms of popular music.

In the meantime, is Mauritius making the most of its traditional dance and music, and doing everything possible to build an archive of sega?

There is a growing realisation that we should record and document more of our recent history before it is too late. A start has already been made with children's games and songs, and the oral history of sega should be recorded before it is lost with the demise of the present generation of elderly Mauritians.

Some of their memories go back to the turn of the century and, in their recollection of stories told them by their own parents and grandparents, they are our last

97

precious link with the nineteenth century and a time when sega was quite untouched by foreign influence.

All this should be recorded for posterity. Who better to start with than the 'father of sega' Alphonse Ravaton. Getting his memories down on tape should be an urgent task for the segatorium.

And we must ask if Mauritius is making the most of its folk-dance and music. The 1990 *fête culturelle* held in honour of P'tit Frère could well become an annual event in Quartier Militaire. This is where Ravaton was born and where he is likely to end his days and it would be a fitting honour to him.

The *fête culturelle* could become a wonderful carnival of sega, a really colourful show that would be welcomed by both Mauritians and tourists. Quartier Militaire would be an ideal setting for this, being at the centre of the island.

Would it be considered too commercial to turn this village into our version of Memphis, Tennessee, the home (or is it now the shrine?) of Elvis Presley? Who knows, a hundred years hence music lovers could be flocking to Quartier Militaire as they do to Salzburg today!

It is only by promoting and selling sega and by fully recognising and honouring the best segatiers that talented young Mauritians will want to get involved and have ambitions to make names for themselves as segatiers. If sega is to survive in its traditional form it must be kept alive and well in its birthplace.

However, if sega is to spread throughout the world it must be promoted overseas as well. There is no doubt that our folk music deserves a worldwide audience. We have seen what success Mauritian singers have had in France and there is no reason why this success should not be repeated in other countries, particularly where many Mauritians have settled.

Sega has a lot to offer and has already proved that it has a wide appeal. Many visitors to Mauritius and people who have heard sega elsewhere are entranced and cannot keep away from it. It has proved to be irresistible as a dance music in almost any surroundings. The demand for sega is surely there.

After its success in France, Britain, the home of the largest expatriate Mauritian community, seems the most likely place for sega to make a big impact. The record-buying youngsters are very cosmopolitan in their outlook and always ready to experiment with different styles of music, and of course English is the language of popular music the world over. The British have discovered the sound of Africa, and are prepared to pay to hear more.

Sega can be packaged in two forms. Firstly, as dance music that is new, exotic and exciting. It has dance steps that disco dancers can learn to do quickly and has the potential to be enormously successful.

Secondly, *séga typique* has all the attributes of good entertainment: rousing music, interesting instruments, colourful and sexy costumes and the dance itself—which tells of pursuit, courtship and fulfilments. It is delightful to watch, and what is more people can join in too, which is much more fun!

Such sega shows, complete with instrumentalists and singers, would make good television and would be a breath of fresh air among dated high-kicking cabaret shows, dancing on ice and pop videos. They would also make ideal entertainment for annual dinners and conferences: most people would find them vastly more enjoyable than after-dinner speakers!

London already has a nucleus of very accomplished sega dancers, for example the winners of the UK Sega Championships and some of the other contestants. Dancers like Sheila Moorghen, Kishnasamy Soobramaney, Jocelyne Constant and Richard Dowlet, to name but a few, already have years of sega dancing behind them. What is needed is a first-rate sega singer.

Probably the sort of singer who could be really successful is someone with whom the youngsters could identify. Babalé could probably fill a concert or dance hall every month if he were to stay in Britain, but it must be admitted that his appeal would be mainly to older Mauritians, not the youngsters.

So sega needs not just a brilliant performer with charm and charisma, but someone sophisticated and cosmopolitan enough to appeal to the younger generation because it is in their hands that the future success of sega lies. Perhaps it is a tall order.

And that is not all. To be internationally successful sega needs good song writers who are really au fait with current trends and idiom, and who can catch the mood of sega as well as express it in English lyrics.

And that brings us to the dilemma: the conflict between the desire to share sega with a wider public while keeping sight of its traditions and history; of moulding and packaging sega so that it appeals to the modern world, without losing its unique charm and individuality.

But it is not impossible. The first requisite is to realise that sega could be much more widely appreciated and played; that it is possible, and indeed desirable, to try to promote sega. There is no reason why sega should not one day become as widely known as jazz and as popular as reggae.

But time is on our side. Sega is not a new phenomenon but goes back to the days when swashbuckling pirates frequented our treasure island. If sega were to achieve international acclaim too quickly we probably would not be able to cope, and we must remember that too meteoric a rise could mean it would be just as quickly forgotten. Sega, hopefully, is here to stay.

# NOTES AND REFERENCES

1. **Bibliography of Mauritius (1502-1954)**, Toussaint & Adolphe (Mauritius Government 1956).

2. **The Origins of Mauritian Words No. 2: Sega**, Philip Baker (*Mauritian International*, No. 4, Oct.-Dec. 1984).

3. The word 'Creole' has a different meaning in Mauritius and the other Mascarene islands to that in other parts of the world. In this region Creole refers to the descendants of the black slaves, and whilst most of them are now of mixed blood and statistically referred to as *population générale*, some are still completely negroid. Our French patois is known as Creole because it was these people who first spoke, indeed created, the language.

   Elsewhere the word applies to the descendants of the early European settlers in former Spanish, French and Portuguese colonies of America, Africa and the East Indies.

   According to **Chambers 20th Century Dictionary**, the word Creole also refers to "native, but of mixed blood: applied to native French or Spanish stock in Louisiana (US)".

   In Mauritius, Creoles with predominantly white blood are known as *mulâtre* (mulatto). People of the French-speaking Caribbean islands now refer to their patois as Creole.

4. **Terms Used in Mauritian Music**, Claudie Ricaud (*Mauritian International*, No. 8, Oct.-Dec. 1985 and No. 9, Jan.-Mar. 1986).

5. Another reference to this instrument in 1834 described it as a harmonica! But since the 1860s it has been known in Mauritius as a *bobre*. Claudie Ricaud *(op. cit.)*.

6. **Dictionary of Mauritian Creole**, P. Baker & V. Hookoomsing (Editions L'Harmattan–Paris 1987).

7. **The Origins of Mauritian Words No. 4: Tamtam**, Philip Baker (*Mauritian International* No. 5, Jan.-Mar. 1985).

8. **Mauritius: The Politics of Change**, A. R. Mannick (Dodo Books –UK 1989).

9. **Paul et Virginie**, Bernardin de Saint-Pierre (Editions Garnier–Paris). Also English translation by John Donovan (Peter Owen–London).

10. **Guide to Mauritius**, Royston Ellis (Bradt Publications UK 1988), has an interesting and well-researched chapter on the district of Rivière Noire.

11. *Case* or *la case* is Creole for a house or any dwelling place.

103